Punishment in Islamic Law:
A Comparative Study

D1598862

Punishment in Islamic Law: A Comparative Study

Mohamed S. El-Awa

Legal Adviser, Arab Bureau of Education
for the Gulf States
Former Associate Professor of Law
University of Riyadh

American Trust Publications
Indianapolis
1982

ISBN No. 0-89259-015-7
Copyright © 1981 by American Trust Publications
10900 West Washington Street
Indianapolis, Indiana 46231 U.S.A.
Library of Congress Catalogue Card Number 80-65482

DEDICATION

This book is dedicated to the memory of the late

Hasan al-Ashmawi,

on whose initiative this study was undertaken, and without whose encouragement and help it would never have been completed.

ACKNOWLEDGEMENTS

This book was originally written as a doctoral thesis, which was submitted to the University of London in May, 1972. The thesis was prepared under the supervision of Professor N.J. Coulson, to whom I am deeply indebted.

I must express my gratitude to my wife, not only for typing the proofs but also for the time she spent with me discussing my ideas and conclusions. I am grateful to the eminent professor of Islamic law, Shaikh Muhammad Mustafa Shalabi, former Head of the Department of Shari'a at the University of Alexandria, Egypt, to whose guidance and teaching I owe my career as a student of Islamic law. Finally, I am thankful to Mrs. Jyl Francis of the School of Oriental and African Studies, University of London, for her efforts in editing the original manuscript.

CONTENTS

INTRODUCTION

All penal systems are concerned, in the first place, with the punishment of the offender. The study of the theory of punishment is, therefore, an essential step in understanding any penal system. At the same time, the application of a particular penal system cannot be justified unless it has become clear that its theory of punishment can successfully achieve the required ends and objectives. Broadly speaking, in Western penal systems the theories of punishment are based on, and justified by, considerations of social utility, while in Islamic law the theory of punishment is based on the belief in the divine revelation contained in the Qur'an and the Sunna of Prophet Muhammad.

The fact is that the Qur'an and Sunna contain very little, if any, theory. Rather, they contain basic rules and commands, usually expressed in a very broad manner and frequently capable of varying interpretations. There are also some specific injunctions and prohibitions, but these are very few and concern a variety of subjects. The formation of theories in Islamic law began at a comparatively later stage, when the schools of Islamic law emerged in the second century after the Hijra and in succeeding centuries.

The writings of the scholars of each school include many volumes dealing with the criminal aspects of the Islamic legal system. Different interpretations of the Qur'an and the Sunna, and diverse views concerning what is good and what is evil, as well as varied social, economic, and political circumstances led to the formation of various legal theories on almost all the legal provisions, including, of course, the penal system.

During the last fifty years, many lawyers who have been trained in modern legal approaches have been gradually attracted to the study of the Islamic penal system. Consequently, a considerable amount of research has been published on various aspects of the subject in several European languages. In many cases the Islamic penal system was either totally rejected or, in other instances, strongly defended on the basis of broad generalities or gross misunderstandings. A careful study analyzing and illustrating the underlying philosophy of the theory of punishment in Islamic law in the light of contemporary approaches to the subject therefore seems necessary. The present study was undertaken with this end in view.

In dealing with the subject, I have divided this work into five chapters. The first is devoted to a discussion of the punishments known as *hudud*, or fixed punishments. Classical treatises classify the punishments of six offences within the category of *hadd*. However, it seems to me that only four of these six offences appear to have been correctly described as *hadd* offences. Accordingly, the second chapter is concerned with the remaining two offences. Here I must point out that some jurists add a seventh offence to the *hadd* category, i.e., the so-called offence of *baghi* or armed resistance to the political authority of the Muslim state. As known to Islamic law, this offence, if it can rightly be so termed, is understood to be committed when a group of Muslims who disagree with the political authority on some matters justify their opposition, although erroneously, on the ground of their dogmatic conviction. If they do not fight the authority, or rather the Muslim community, they are not to be attacked, while if they do, only such defence as is necessary to defeat them is permissible. For this reason, I consider the treatment of the *bughat* to fall under the doctrine of legitimate defence or *daf' al-sa'il*, a topic with which this research is not concerned. Consequently no reference has been made to the treatment of the *bughat*; a brief account of it, however, may be found in the *Encyclopaedia of Islam* (II, p. 828).

The third chapter deals with the Islamic approach to the punishments for homicide and injury. In dealing with this topic, I will show that the place given to the personal rights of the victim or his relatives is the main feature of the Islamic concept of retaliation or *qisas*. An attempt has therefore been made to elucidate this point, especially with reference to the right of relatives to waive the punishment.

The fourth chapter deals with the concept of *ta'zir* or discretionary punishments. Since the Islamic penal system recognizes only four or, according to the classical authorities, six offences for which a fixed punishment is prescribed, discretionary punishments have a very important place. The philosophy underlying this concept and its general principles has not been treated with the attention it deserves. Recent works on the subject have enabled me to deal more specifically with it, particularly in the context of the place of this concept in the general theory of penal law and its role in protecting and enforcing the moral values of Islam.

Throughout my research, I have felt the need to say something about the methods of proof relating to criminal cases in Islamic law. According ly, I have devoted the fifth and last chapter to explaining, although briefly, the law of evidence in criminal cases.

In writing on any Islamic topic, one must overcome many difficulties, two of which are worth mentioning. The first is the task of collecting the relevant material from the enormously vast body of available sources of each school of law, a particularly difficult job since the jurists' methods of writing require a good deal of orientation and familiarity with the expressions and possible headings under which they might have dealt with one problem or another. In the main, I have concentrated on the four Sunni schools, i.e., the Hanafi, Maliki, Shafi'i', and Hanbali. The views of the Zahiri school are often mentioned, but I have omitted the Shi'is except in some cases where the Zaydis views have been referred to. However, it must be mentioned that as far as the theory of punishment is concerned, all schools agree as to the main principles and the concepts underlying them. The differences of opinion appear only in the details of their interpretation and application.

The second difficulty is that of translation from Arabic to English, especially with respect to the Qur'an and Hadith. As for the Qur'an, many translations were consulted, and some necessary changes were made. But it must be remembered that, to quote Professor Arberry "the Qur'an (like all other literary masterpieces) is untranslatable." As for the Hadith, the translation of *Mishkat al-Masabih* by Fazlul Karim was very helpful, but many amendments had to be made in using it.

Bearing in mind the fact that in writing about the Islamic penal system, Muslims are generally either apologists or opponents, I have tried my best to be objective in dealing with the various topics contained in this work. The views expressed here may not all be unanimously agreed upon, but I have always tried to support those which I thought to be harmonious with the spirit of Islam.

Finally, in discussing punishment, and especially the Islamic concept of it, one may quote Professor Blanshard's statement that "punishment is unpleasant to inflict and not particularly pleasant to discuss. But we clearly need to discuss it."

CHAPTER I

The Fixed Punishments *(Al-Hudud)*

According to the classical manuals of Islamic law, Islamic criminal law recognizes six major offences, each of which has a penalty prescribed in fixed terms in the Qur'an or the Sunna. These offences are known to Muslim jurists as the offences of *hudud*.[1]

I. Definition

In Islamic law all duties and obligations are divided into two categories: one is known as *haqq Allah,* and the other as *haqq adami.* As used in the Islamic legal sense, the word *hadd* (plural, *hudud*) means a punishment which has been prescribed by God in the revealed text of the Qur'an or the Sunna, the application of which is the right of God or *haqq Allah*.[2]

In the penal context, a punishment which is classified as *haqq Allah* embodies three main aspects. The first is that this punishment is prescribed in the public interest; the second is that it cannot be lightened nor made heavier; and the third is that, after being reported to the judge, it is not to be pardoned either by him, by the political authority, or by the victim of the offence.[3] The unchangeability of the *hadd* punishment is supported by the interpretation of the Qur'anic verse, "These are the limits of Allah. Do not transgress them."[4] The third feature of the *hadd* punishment is based on a hadith reported by Bukhari and Muslim, to which reference will be made shortly.[5]

II. Classification

The six offences generally recognized as offences of *hudud* are the drinking of alcohol, theft, armed robbery, illicit sexual relations, slander-

1

ous accusation of unchastity, and apostasy. Apart from retaliation or *qisas*, which is the punishment for homicide and injury, in the Islamic penal system all other offences are punishable by discretionary punishments known as *ta'zir*. However, to classify an offence in the category of *hadd*, it must be established that the punishment for it is determined in fixed terms in the Qur'an or the Sunna.

Although the majority of jurists agree on the classification of the aforementioned offences, some authorities hold differing views, either adding to these six offences or reducing their number.[6] Taking into consideration that a *hadd* punishment is a punishment defined by God in the Qur'an or the Sunna, it appears to me that only four of the six mentioned offences can be classifed as offences of *hudud*. The remaining two, namely apostasy and alcohol-drinking, cannot be so classifed since neither of them warrants a punishment which has been strictly defined in the words of the Qur'an or the Sunna. This chapter will therefore be devoted to discussing the four *hadd* punishments for theft, armed robbery, illicit sexual relations, and slanderous accusation of unchastity.

Although this work is primarily concerned with the principles underlying the Islamic concept of punishment, the jurists' traditional pattern in dealing with these categories of punishments will be followed in order to illustrate the kind of punishment prescribed for each offence and what conduct constitutes this offence.

III. The Punishment for Theft (al-Sariqa)

The punishment for theft is prescribed in the Qur'anic verse, "As for thieves, both male and female, cut off their hands. It is the recompense of their own deeds, an exemplary punishment from Allah . . ."(V:38).[7]

As reported in Bukhari and Muslim, this punishment was practiced by the Prophet himself. He cut off the thief's hand and also ordered the amputation of a female thief's hand.[8] In the same tradition the Prophet prohibited any mediation in executing the *hudud*.[9] From this latter report jurists have deduced the rule that no *hadd* punishment is remissible, a rule which characterizes this category of punishment and distinguishes it from both *ta'zir* or discretionary punishments, for both *ta'zir* and *qisas* may be remitted even after being reported to the judge.

The jurists have defined theft as "taking someone else's property by stealth."[10] There is almost complete agreement on this definition among jurists, but they are not so unanimous concerning the value of the stolen property, how the hand should be cut off, and the question of the places from which property is stolen, i.e., the problem of custody. These are the main points of controversy regarding the offence of theft with which we will deal here.

III. 1. The Value of the Stolen Property (*Nisab al-Sariqa*)

According to the majority of jurists, the value of the stolen property should exceed, or at least be worth, a minimum fixed by the law; the punishment for theft is not to be inflicted if its value is less than this minimum. The schools of Islamic law differ on the determination of this minimum.

According to the Hanafi school, the punishment for theft cannot be inflicted unless the value of the stolen property is ten dirhams or more. The jurists support this view, on the one hand, by the alleged hadith which states, "No amputation is due unless for ten dirhams." On the other hand, they claim that the consensus (*ijma*) holds that for ten dirhams or more the punishment should be inflicted, while for less then ten dirhams there are differing opinions. Thus, there is doubt about the legality of inflicting the punishment for such value, and in cases of doubt, the *hadd* punishment cannot be applied.[11]

According to the Maliki school, the punishment can be inflicted for stealing property valued at three dirhams or a fourth of a dinar. That is, this school maintains, the value for which the Prophet inflicted the punishment for theft, as did Othman b. Affan, the third caliph.[12] At the same time Malik draws a parallel between the minimum amount of dower and the minimum value of the stolen property. He is reported to have said, "I do not think that a woman should be married for a dower of less than one-fourth of a dinar, and this is the minimum value for which the hand is to be amputated." Hence, by way of analogy (*qiyas*), Malik fixed the minimum value at one-fourth of a dinar.[13]

The Hanbali school holds the same view as the Maliki, but its justification rests on the basis of *ahadith* and not on analogy.[14]

According to the Shafi'i school, the minimum value of the stolen property should be one-quarter of a dinar; it established that a dinar was twelve dirhams in the Prophet's time, and hence three dirhams were equal to a quarter of a dinar.[15] Thus, the three schools, the Maliki, Shafi'i and Hanbali, hold the same view concerning the minimum value of the stolen property, while the Hanafi school raised the value to ten dirhams. The Shi'i school of the Zaydis holds the same view on the matter as the Hanafi.[16]

On the other hand, the Zahiri school, represented by Ibn Hazm in his book *Al-Muhalla*, holds a view according to which there is no fixed minimum value for stolen property. For gold the minimum value is held to be one-quarter of a dinar,[17] while for everything else the punishment should be inflicted when the value of the property is equal to the value of a shield *(turs)*, since this was the value for which the Prophet inflicted the punishment for theft.[18] But Ibn Hazm did not fix the value of the *turs*, and it is clear that it is to be fixed according to custom or *'urf*.

The purpose of the jurists' attempts to determine the minimum value of stolen property was to avoid the infliction of the very severe *hadd* punishment for theft unless the stolen property was of considerable value. All the schools agree that if the stolen property is worthless this punishment should not be inflicted. The culprit will still be liable to a *ta'zir* punishment, but not to the *hadd* prescribed for the crime of *sariqa*.[19]

It should be noted that all these discussions are only of historical value today. This seems obvious when we take into account the fluctuation in the value of money and the amount considered negligible under given circumstances, e.g., from one society to another and from one time to another. Consequently, no rule can be taken over from any of the schools of Islamic law and applied today. It is the duty of the lawmakers in each country to decide the minimum value in respect to which the punishment is to be applied.

Some may argue that this does not accord with the Prophet's determination of the minimum value of the stolen property, and therefore it cannot be accepted within Islamic law. In reply, one can say that this determination was based upon what suited the Prophetic community. It may also have been suitable for one or two centuries after the Prophet's time, but not today. There are many instances of changing details which do not serve a particular purpose after they were shaped by the Prophet or even by the Qur'an itself. Generally, any decision based on grounds of the public interest *(maslaha)*[20] can be changed according to the change in circumstances.[21] This is a firmly established rule among the Muslim jurists who formulated the priniples of Islamic law known as *usul al-fiqh*.[22]

With regard to this question, Ibn al-Qayyim stated that the reason for considering one-quarter of a dinar as the minimum value was that this amount was sufficient for the daily maintenance of an average man.[23] Since this is the case, it is clear that the determination of one quarter of a dinar as the minimum value of the stolen property was based on social circumstances which are certainly variable. This determination may, therefore, be reviewed in the light of contemporary social circumstances. Furthermore, the gold coins used in the Prophet's time, in terms of which this minimum value was fixed, are no longer in use. This also justifies the need to review the minimum value.

III. 2. How the Hand Should Be Cut Off *(Makan al-Qati')*

On this point there are three main views among the jurists. Nearly all of them agree that the thief's right hand should be amputated from the wrist for the first theft.[24] But they differ in respect to subsequent thefts. According to the four Sunni schools, if there is a second theft the thief's left foot should be amputated. The Hanafis hold that for subsequent thefts there should be no further amputation, and that the only way to punish the offender is by *ta'zir*.[25]

On the other hand, the Malikis, Shafi'is and Ahmad b. Hanbal hold the view that for the third theft, the left hand should be cut off, and for the fourth, the right foot.[26]

The third view was expressed by Ibn Hazm in *Al-Muhalla*. He claimed that the Qur'anic verse previously cited allowed no amputation except the thief's hands. Thus, according to Ibn Hazm's understanding of this verse, in the second theft the left hand should be cut off, while for subsequent thefts there should be no further amputations.[27]

The Zaydi school held the same view as the Hanafi school, as did Ibn Qudamah of the Hanbali school.[28]

At the same time, it is related that Ibn 'Abbas and 'Ata' allowed the thief's right hand to be cut off for the first theft, and nothing but *ta'zir* to be applied for subsequent thefts.[29] When 'Ata' was asked about the second theft, he insisted that no further *hadd* punishment could be inflicted after the amputation of the right hand for the first theft. He supported his view by citing the Qur'anic verse, "And your Lord was never forgetful,"[30] that is, if God had wanted anything else to be cut off, He would have mentioned it.

In my opinion this latter view is nearest to the spirit of Islamic law. As a contemporary scholar has stated, "The aim behind this sanction is retribution (or deterrence), and this can be easily achieved by indicating that it is applicable . . . ."[31] By adding to this Ibn Hazm's statement that we should not go beyond what is prescribed in the Qur'an and Sunna in relation to this punishment,[32] one can say that the *hadd* punishment for theft is the cutting off of the thief's right hand for the first theft. In the event of his committing a subsequent theft, he becomes liable to a *ta'zir* punishment, which will be explained later. This interpretation can be supported by the well-known rule that "every crime for which there is no *hadd* renders its perpetrator liable to *ta'zir*."[33] Moreover, nothing can be added to the retributive or deterrent function of the punishment by applying the majority's views and amputating other limbs.

Finally, it is necessary to mention the Maliki view that the thief's hand should be amputated from the elbow.[34] However, this view is unacceptable to all the other jurists, and it cannot find any support either in the practice of the Prophet and his followers or in the usage of the word hand (*yad*) as it is understood in Arabic.[35]

III. 3. The Question of Custody (al-Hirz)

Stolen property is property taken illegally from its owner. Owners usually keep their goods in a proper place in which they are safe. The storage place, or the custody of the goods, is known to Muslim jurists as *hirz*. The disagreement relative to this topic centers on the question of whether the taking of the property may be classified as theft if, at the time of its taking, it was not in its proper place. The four Sunni and the Zaydi schools are unanimous in agreeing that in order to consider the taking of someone else's property as a theft, it must be proved that this property was being kept in its proper place (*hirzu mithlih*).[36]

The Zahiri school, on the other hand, disagrees with this view, holding that the taking of property belonging to others is a theft even if the property in question was not being kept in its proper place.[37]

The majority view is supported by a *hadith* in which the Prophet did not allow the *hadd* punishment to be imposed unless the stolen goods were taken from their *hirz*. This *hadith* is regarded as authentic by the majority, while the Zahiri school considers it false. The debate, therefore, centers on whether this *hadith* should be classified as false or otherwise. This *hadith*, it should be pointed out, was narrated by Malik in *Al-Muwatta'*, and is classified as authentic by the scholars of *Hadith*.[38] Accordingly, the view of the majority is the one to be supported.

It should be mentioned, however, that what is considered as a *hirz*, or proper place for keeping something, is determined according to custom or *'urf*. Hence it may change from one locality to another and from one time to another.[39] In view of this, the jurists debated such matters as the classification of stealing from the public treasury *(bayt al-mal)*, embezzlement *(ikhtilas)*, and stealing from a mosque or public bathroom, etc. All these questions arose because the custom in a given locality or at a given time was different from that of another locality or time. These matters should, therefore, be considered with reference to the given circumstances of the time, and nothing should be taken over from the juristic writings.

To sum up, the amputation of the thief's hand as the *hadd* punishment for theft is to be imposed only when the stolen property reaches a minimum value and has been taken from its proper place of custody or *hirz*. When one of these two conditions is not proved, the offender, although not liable to the *hadd* punishment, may nevertheless be liable to a punishment within the category of *ta'zir*.

IV. Armed Robbery *(al-Hiraba)*

Three terms are used for this crime: *al-Hiraba* or Armed Robbery, *al-Sariqa al-Kubra* or the Great Theft, and *Qat' al-Tariq* or Highway Robbery. The three terms are used interchangeably by the jurists and in the books of *fiqh*.[40] In my view, the first term, *al-Hiraba*, is preferable as it expresses the spirit of the crime as mentioned in the relevant verses of the Qur'an.

In passing, it may be noted that the difference between the crime of theft and the crime of armed robbery appears in the basic element of each crime. As mentioned before, in theft the basic element is the taking of someone else's property by stealth. Conversely, in armed robbery it is the intention to take property by force. Accordingly, the culprit in the latter case is liable to punishment even without actually having brought the intended crime to completion, e.g., theft, killing of passers-by, etc.[41] In other words, to lie in wait on travelled highways with the intention of committing this crime constitutes a complete crime in itself.

There are many definitions of this crime in the books of *fiqh*. The most comprehensive of them defines it as "waiting by the way (or highway) to steal travellers' property by force and by this means obstructing travel on this road."[42]

The punishment for this crime is in the *hadd* category. As is stated in the Qur'an: "The only recompense for those who make war upon God and His Messenger and strive after corruption in the land will be that they will be killed, or crucified, or have their hands and feet cut off on alternate sides, or will be expelled from the land. Such will be their recompence in this world, and in the Hereafter theirs will be an awful punishment, except those who repent before you overpower them. For know that God is Forgiving, Merciful" (V:33-34).

It is reported that in the Prophet's time a group of people from the tribes of 'Ukal and 'Urayana came to Madina and subsequently fell ill. The Prophet advised them to go to the place where the camels were grazing. After their recovery, they brutally killed the camels' guard and took the camels. The Prophet sent some of his companions after them and the malefactors were captured. Then he punished them by cutting off their hands and feet and gouging out their eyes, exactly as they had done to the camels' guard.[43]

There are two views concerning the link between this case and the above Qur'anic verses. First, some commentators on the Qur'an claim that this case was dealt with solely according to the Prophet's own decision and the Qur'anic verses were later revealed to show him his mistake in exceeding the punishment stated in the Qur'an.[44] The other view, which is held by the majority of the jurists, is that these verses were revealed after the carrying out the punishment in question to indicate its correctness.[45] Other punishments which are not mentioned in the Qur'an were carried out according to some general rules of the Qur'an, such as ". . . and one who attacks you, attack him in the same manner as he attacked you" (II:194), and "The recompence for an evil deed is a similar evil" (XL:11-40).[46] However, it is interesting to note that some jurists, and even some Western writers, understood the punishment of *hiraba* mentioned in the Qur'anic verses and executed in the case of the people of 'Ukal and 'Urayna by the Prophet to be the punishment for apostasizing from Islam. This view will be discussed later. It is only necessary to indicate here in passing that the preferred, if not the only accepted, view among the jurists is that this punishment is to be applied only in cases of *hiraba*.[47]

The jurists are divided about some matters related to the crime of *hiraba*. We will limit this study to three of the controversial points only: the possibility of committing the crime in a town or village,[48] the problem of the carrying out of the punishment, and the execution of the punishment of banishment *(nafi)*.

IV. 1. The Site of Commission of *Hiraba*

According to Abu Hanifa, the founder of the Hanafi school, what is termed armed robbery can be committed only on the highway *(al-tariq)*. In other words, a similar crime committed in a town or a village where the victims can be helped will not be considered as *hiraba*. Sarakhsi, in supporting this view, claimed that the designation of the crime, *qat' al-tari*, implies this conclusion. Hence, the punishment for it cannot be inflicted unless the crime is committed in an uninhabited place.[49]

However, according to the Maliki, Shafi'i', Zahiri, Zaydi, and Imami schools, the *hadd* punishment is applicable wherever this criminal act is committed.[50] The jurists of the Hanbali school are divided between this and the above mentioned opinion, for Ahmad b. Hanbal gave no answer when was asked concerning this point. Due to this, some Hanbali jurists hold a view similar to that of Abu Hanifa, but others embrace the contrary view.[51]

Some jurists formulate this condition in different words; they consider it to be *hiraba* if the victims of this crime, even when they ask for help, cannot be assisted.[52] It would appear that they were led to this formulation because they thought it to be in line with the nature of the crime. And if this view is examined, it will be seen that a crime of this type contains an important element which separates it from ordinary theft. That is to say, it can only be committed with disregard to the public order and the security of the community.[53] This element can be found both in the committing of a crime on the travellers' road or far from a place in which help can reach the victims, as well as in the committing of it in a town or village, or in a place where help can be found.

A very similar conclusion concerning the committing of this crime in a town was reached by Shafi'i in his work *Al-Umm*.[54] As for the possibility of helping the victims, it is sufficient to note that the first case in which the punishment for *hiraba* was applied was a case in which help could have reached them. Hence there is no room for such a condition.[55] It can therefore be said that no special consideration should be given to the place where the crime is committed, for if a person who commits a crime in a town is not of more dangerous character than the one who commits it elsewhere, he certainly cannot be considered to be less so.[56]

IV. 2.   The Carrying-Out of the Punishments *(Tanfidh al-'Uqubat)*

The previously cited Qur'anic verse prescribed four punishments for the crime of *hiraba*, i.e., death, crucifixion, cutting off the hands and feet on the opposite sides (the right hand and the left foot or vice versa), and banishment *(nafi)*. The jurists differ concerning the infliction of these punishments. Since banishment will be discussed later in more detail, we will here examine their views concerning the other three punishments.

There is almost complete agreement among the jurists that the death penalty is to be inflicted by the sword,[57] but this method of carrying out the punishment should be discussed as well. It may be argued that any other method of execution would be unacceptable because of the existing consensus or *ijma'*. But this is a faulty argument because this consensus basically expressed the jurists' view that the common method of execution in their time constituted the proper way of inflicting capital punishment. When this method becomes outmoded, it need not be insisted upon as the only way of implementing the punishment. It is again a question of changing the decision in accordance with the change in what it was based upon,[58] for as was said earlier, any decision which was based on public interest *(maslaha)* or on custom *('urf)* should be changed when circumstances change.[59]

As for crucifixion, there are two opinions among the Sunni schools. The first is that the criminal should be crucified alive and then be thrust by a javelin. This view is held by the Hanafi school and by Ibn al-Qasim of the Maliki school.[60] The second view is that the criminal should first be executed in the usual manner and his body should subsequently be crucified for three days as warning and deterrent to others. This view is held by the Shafi'i and the Hanbali schools and by some of the Maliki jurists.[61] According to Ibn Hazm, crucifixion is a separate punishment which should not be inflicted in conjunction with any other punishment, whether before or after it. Hence, if the judge chooses to impose this punishment, the criminal should be crucified alive, left until he dies, and then taken down and buried.[62]

The main element in the prescription of crucifixion, in my view, is to prevent the commission of this grave crime by the threat of unusual punishment. Moreover, as Ibn Hazm stated, the Qur'anic verse cited does not mention that crucifixion should be used after or in conjunction with execution. Finally, if, as I believe, deterrence or prevention is the fundamental element in prescribing this punishment, there is no point in adding execution to crucifixion when crucifixion is sufficient to attain this primary objective.

With due regard to these three points, I am of the opinion that this punishment is a completely separate one. It is also noteworthy that Malik, when asked about it, did not reply but merely said, "I have never heard of anyone who was crucified except a man called al-Harith who was crucified in the time of Abd al-Malik b. Marwan after claiming to be a prophet."[63]

This observation of Malik's gives me the impression that this punishment was prescribed solely to deter the potential criminal. This impression is confirmed by the fact that although this is the most severe of all punishments, the Prophet did not impose it upon the people of 'Ukal and 'Urayna. In a contemporary text, a writer has compared this punishment to death by shooting under the military law of some countries,[64] claiming that these are nearly the same punishment, but this view is far from correct because the differences between the two kinds of punishment are so clear that they cannot be compared.

Finally, in the texts of Islamic law, we find lengthy discussions about the order of inflicting the punishments prescribed in the Qur'anic verses previously cited. To summarize these discussions, one can divide the jurists into two groups. The Maliki and Zahiri schools hold that the judge has the right to choose the punishment suitable in each case and to impose it.[65] To explain this freedom of choice, al-Qarafi stated that the judge has to do his best to determine what is most beneficial for the community and then to act on it.[66]

On the other hand, the Hanafi, Shafi'i, and Hanbali schools deny the judge this authority, holding that this crime involves more than one possible punishment, depending on the manner in which the criminal act is committed. Thus, if the criminal kills his victim, he should be sentenced to death; if he steals his money, he should have his right hand and left foot cut off; and if he threatens travellers, he should be banished. In other words, the imposition of the punishments is to differ according to the nature of the crime and not according to the nature of the personal character of the criminal.[67] This last statement indicates that the two views are the outcome of different approaches. The jurists who hold the first view differentiate between punishments in consideration of the personal character of the criminal,[68] while others justify the application of one punishment or the other in consideration of the actual offence committed.

IV. 3. Banishment *(al-Nafi)*

There are three views in Sunni schools concerning this punishment. The Hanafi view is that banishment signifies imprisonment;[69] the Maliki school understands it as imprisonment in another country, not in that of the criminal;[70] and the Sh afi'i and Hanbali schools claim that the meaning of the word "*nafi*" is the pursuing of the criminal from country to country if he escapes.[71]

In reviewing the various points of view it can be said that the view of the Shafi'i and Hanbali schools is not supported by any evidence, and that of the Hanafi school seems to be the most acceptable. The Malikis, by adding to imprisonment the condition that it should be outside the criminal's own country, try to apply the word *nafi* in both senses. There is, however, no need to do this since imprisonment is a separate punishment which is known independently of the Qur'anic usage. In this context the word *nafi* (banishment) and not the word *habs* (imprisonment) is used in the Qur'an. In any case, the culprit is to be punished by banishment until he gives evidence of a better character and does not seem likely to again engage in criminal behavior, or, in the jurists' words, until his repentance is proved.[72] This principle is comparable, to some extent, to the parole system introduced in England by the Criminal Justice Act of 1967.[73]

At this point, two questions still remain unanswered. The first is the common argument that it is hard to imagine that a prophet could prescribe such a cruel punishment. This agrument has been dealt with by one of the most distinguished scholars of Islamic law, the late Egyptian judge, 'Abd al-Qadir 'Uda. In his previously mentioned book, he replies to this question by comparing the punishment for *hiraba* with that of imprisonment in modern penal systems. 'Uda points out the well known fact that most prisoners who are released from jail are dangerous individuals, often expert in methods of committing crime without being caught. He then asks if anyone can claim that a man with only a single hand and foot can be a danger to society. Since the aim of this punishment is solely retribution, he continues, this is the best punishment to serve such an end.[74] However, another contemporary scholar of Islamic law employed another approach to refute this argument. Shaikh Muhammad Abu Zahra, in his previously mentioned book, explains that the aim of both Islamic law, as well as the sacred Jewish law contained in the Torah, is to achieve public security and peace for the community as well as retribution for the criminal minority; accordingly, the necessary means for the attainment of this latter end were prescribed both in the Torah and the Qur'an.[75]

The second question concerns the law of pardon for offenders who repent and whether the punishment for *hiraba* should be considered a dead letter because of this law. To answer this question, one should again bear in mind that this punishment, and indeed all the *hudud* punishments in the Islamic penal system, are prescribed mainly to protect society from crime. In order to achieve this purpose, Islamic law, while prescribing punishments for criminals, makes it possible for them to be pardoned when they realize the evil of their conduct and desire to mend their ways.

This does not contradict the earlier quotation from Abu Zahra. While punishment may be withheld, provision must be made for all the injuries and harm resulting from the criminal's act.[76] In this way, society does not lose anything. On the contrary, it gains a new member who, if he had not been given the chance to repent, forever would have been considered an outlaw.

V. Illicit Sexual Relations *(Al-Zina)*

Generally speaking, in modern penal systems voluntary sexual relationships outside marriage are not considered a crime. Such sexual freedom is completely unknown to all the sacred laws. The Jewish, the Christian, and the Islamic laws all forbid, and render punishable, all types of sexual relations outside marriage. The differences between these laws appear in what are considered unlawful and punishable sexual relations, and the punishments prescribed for the prohibited practices. In this section we shall discuss these different laws.

In Islamic law the definition of *zina* as a crime differs from one school to another. The most comprehensive definition is that given by the Hanafi school: "Sexual intercourse between a man and a woman without legal right or without the semblance of legal right (*al-milk* or *shubhat al-milk*)."[77] It should be pointed out that in Arabic the same term, *zina*, applies both to adultery (defined as illicit sexual relations between two married individuals) and fornication, i.e., sexual relations between an unmarried man and woman.

In spite of all the differences in defining the crime of *zina* among the schools of Islamic law, all jurists agree that the main element in this crime is unlawful intercourse. Hence, any sexual relationship between a man and a woman which does not involve intercourse is not punishable by the *hadd* punishment. These relations cannot be considered legal (*mubah*); on the contrary, they are prohibited (*haram*), but their punishment is in the category of *ta'zir*. The *hadd* punishment for *zina* should not be applied in such cases.[78]

The punishment for the crime of *zina* is prescribed in the following Qur'anic verse: "The committers of *zina*, male and female, flog each of them with a hundred stripes, and do not let pity for the two withhold you from obedience to God, if you believe in God and the Day of Judgment. And let a party of believers witness their punishment." (XXIV:2)

This is the last verse to be revealed concerning the crime of *zina*, after the earlier revelation of the two verses in Surah IV: "As for those of your women who are guilty of lewdness, call to witness four of you against them. And if they testify (to the truth of the allegation), then confine them to their houses until death takes them or (until) God appoints for them a way (through new legislation). And as for the two of you (males) who are guilty of it, punish them both . . . ."[79]

According to these verses, the punishment for an adulteress was imprisonment in her family's house until she died or until another piece of legislation came into force. For a man who committed the same crime, a bodily punishment was ordered.[80] But soon afterwards another piece of legislation was revealed in the previously-cited verses of Surah XXIV which prescribed one hundred lashes for the unmarried male and female who commit fornication, together with the punishment prescribed by the Sunna for the married male or female, i.e., stoning to death. According to the view of the majority, the punishment prescribed

in IV:15-16 was abrogated after the new legislation,[81] but ac~
Mujahid, a companion of Ibn 'Abbas, it is still applicable in cas~
homosexuality.[82]

However, it is clear that the punishment for *zina* was at first a sort of
ta'zir and it became a *hadd* punishment later, with the form of *hadd* varying according to the marital status of the culprit.

This is agreed upon by all the Muslim jurists, with the sole exception
of the Khariji group of al-Azariqa, who denied that stoning to death was
the punishment for married offenders.[83] The above consensus was always
respected until comparatively recently, when some writers denied that
stoning to death was an applicable punishment, claiming that it had been
cancelled by the revelation of the above-mentioned verses in Surah
XXIV.[84] The evidence on which they relied for their view needs to be
examined. We will discuss this view first, explain the nature of this punishment in its dual aspects, and then deal with the distinction between a
married culprit *(muhsan)* and one who is unmarried *(ghair muhsan)*.

V. 1. Stoning as a Punishment *(al-Rajm)*

According to the majority, the punishment of stoning is prescribed by
the Sunna, but it is reported that a Qur'anic verse was revealed prescribing
this punishment. Again, according to the majority, the text of this
verse was abrogated but its verdict continued to be applied.[85]

It is also narrated that the Prophet ordered this punishment to be carried out in four cases, in one of which the criminals were a male and a
female of the Jewish community of al-Madina.[86] It is controversial, however, whether the Prophet ordered these two Jews to be stoned according
to their own law or according to Islamic law.[87] But in the other three cases,
it is clear that there was no reason to apply the Jewish law since all the
criminals were Muslims.

Those who deny that the punishment of *zina* is stoning support their
view on the following grounds:[88]

i. The abrogation of the words of a Qur'anic verse and the continuity
of its verdict is a controversial point; hence it cannot be of any help to
claim that the Qur'an prescribed stoning as a punishment.

ii. It is possible that the Prophet had the Jews guilty of *zina* stoned
according to their own law; then as there were no revelations concerning
the offence, he had the same punishment inflicted upon the guilty
Muslims.

iii. It is also possible that this punishment was prescribed by the Qur'an, as is related, but that it was abrogated afterwards.

iv. Al-Bukhari related that someone asked Ibn Abi-Awfa, a companion of the Prophet, if the Prophet had ordered stoning to be carried out before or after the prescription of one hundred lashes in Surah XXIV, and Ibn Abi-Awfa replied that he did not know which it was.[89]

As for the abrogated Qur'anic verse, what was said concerning it is correct. One can also add that in some of the *ahadith* concerning this verse, 'Umar asked the Prophet to allow him to write it but the Prophet refused, and this is in itself an evidence of its abrogation.[90] But the point is not that this punishment was prescribed by the Qur'an at all but that it was actually prescribed in the Sunna. Muslim, in his *Sahih*,[91] and the authors of the books of *sunan, ashab al-sunan*, i.e., Abu Dawud, Ibn Majah, al-Nasa'i, al-Timidhi, and al-Bayhaqi, as well as Ahmad b. Hanbal in his *Musnad*, all reported that the Prophet received the revelation (*wahy*) and then told his companions that a new piece of legislation had been revealed to him, namely, that a married male or female should be given one hundred lashes and then stoned to death, while an unmarried male or female should be given one hundred lashes and then banished for one year.[92] Thus, based on this *hadith*, all the jurists implemented the punishment of stoning. It is true that not all of them are in agreement on the flogging of the married culprit or the banishment of one who is unmarried.[93] But this disagreement exists because when the Prophet ordered the punishment of stoning to be carried out, he did not order flogging to precede it, nor did he order banishment with the flogging except in one case in which banishment is claimed to have been based on the public interest.[94] This disagreement, however, does not affect the main point on which there is complete agreement, namely, the punishment of stoning for the married offender.

As for the second and third possibilities, these are mere assumptions and there is no evidence to support them. Particularly in relation to the third case, it is hard to imagine that this punishment could have been abrogated without any knowledge of it on the part of any of the Companions. Such a supposition might obviously lead to a claim of abrogation of every rule in Islamic law.

As for the tradition of Ibn Abi-Awfa, it does not provide any evidence to support the view of those who denied it. All one finds in this tradition is that Ibn Abi-Awfa did not know if the Prophet's imposition of the punishment in question was before or after the revelation of the verses in Surah XXIV. But this does not mean that the punishment was abrogated especially when one knows that the Prophet's companions imposed the same punishment later.[95] Accordingly, one can state that the punishment of stoning to death is prescribed by the Sunna and not by the Qur'an. Moreover, it is the only *hadd* punishment, as far as I know, which is prescribed by the Sunna.

It is noteworthy in this connection that stoning to death was prescribed in the Torah as a punishment for several crimes, among them adultery.[96] Consequently, it may be argued that the Prophet of Islam added this punishment to Islamic law by borrowing it from Jewish law. But the similarity between the two systems of law can rather be understood from the fact that both are divine laws. Since the source of both is God's revelation, it can rightly be expected that many rules in both of them will be similar. This fact of similarity, instead of being used as evidence of Muhammad's borrowing from the Jewish law, can rather be used as evidence of the divine nature of Islamic law. The differences between Jewish and Islamic laws are undeniable, but this is simply because of the different circumstances in which each law was revealed. In other words, in respect to the changeable aspects, the divine law underwent changes from Moses to Muhammad, but with regard to what is unalterable, the law remained the same.[97]

V. 2. The Nature of the Punishment for *Zina*

Among surviving penal systems, that of Islam is unique in its punishment of adultery. It is true that this punishment was prescribed in Jewish law, but it is no longer applied nor is there any suggestion that it may be enforced again. The only explanation for the prescription of such a punishment may be found in the fact that Islamic law, or rather Islam itself, is based entirely on morality. Any moral transgression is seriously condemned by means of severe punishments. In a legal system in which "all acts and relationships are measured by a scale of moral evaluation,"[98] it is natural to find such a deep concern for enforcing sexual morality. The same condition prevailed under Jewish law in which, to quote the *Jewish Encyclopaedia*, "law and morality went hand in hand to prevent the commission of the crime."[99] The desire to protect public morality and to safeguard it against corruption by publicizing the offence, is the reason for limiting the methods of proof to the offender's own confession or to the testimony of four adult male Muslims who have actually witnessed the act of sexual intercourse.[100]

On the other hand, the widest publicity should be given to the implementation of the punishments in order to deter potential offenders. This can be understood from the rule that all punishments, especially that of adultery, should be carried out in public, or, as the Qur'an commands, "let a party of believers witness their punishment" (XXIV:2).[101]

The connection between the Islamic penal system and the moral values of the Muslim Society is the main factor behind many punishments and prohibitions in Islam, but the clearest effect of this connection appears in regard to the punishment for *zina*. More will be said concerning this in the third chapter when we discuss *ta'zir* punishments.

In view of modern ideas concerning personal freedom, and in particular sexual freedom, the Islamic treatment of the offence of *zina* appears very unusual. Here it would be well to recall that the Islamic concept of personal freedom is entirely opposed to that of the post-war generation in the West. Personal freedom, according to the Islamic concept, is permissible only in respect to matters not regulated by the injunctions and prohibitions laid down in the Qur'an and the Sunna, which are expressions of the Divine Will. By contrast, the imposition of such limitation by the supreme Authority is completely absent from the contemporary Western image of the relationship between law, society, and the individual. This different sense of the source of authority may explain many of the differences between the Islamic and Western legal systems.

V. 3. The Distinction Between Married *(Muhsan)* and Unmarried *(Ghair-Muhsan)*

As we have seen, the stoning punishment determined by the Sunna is the punishment for a married male or female who has committed the crime of *zina*, while the punishment for an unmarried male or female, prescribed by the Qur'an, is one hundred lashes. There is consensus on this matter, but, nevertheless, there are two points on which agreement is lacking. These are flogging before stoning for a married culprit and exile for one year for the unmarried culprit after being flogged.

With regard to the married culprit, the Hanafi, Maliki, and Shafi'i schools allow only the stoning of the culprit, since flogging before stoning was abrogated.[102] The Hanbali, Zahiri, and Zaydi schools hold that a married culprit *(muhsan)* should be flogged first and then stoned to death.[103] These schools support their views by a *hadith* related by Muslim and other compilers of the *Hadith* in which the Prophet prescribed both punishments for a *muhsan*. But it is clear enough from the statement of Shafi'i in his book *Al-Risalah* that this prescription of two punishments was afterwards abrogated by the Prophet himself.[104]

As for the unmarried offender, all the schools, except the Hanafi consider the punishment for an unmarried culprit *(ghair-muhsan)* to consist of two parts: one hundred lashes and one year's banishment *(taghrib)*; the books of *fiqh* contain detailed discussions concerning this punishment.[105] But here it is enough to say that the majority view is preferable because the evidence for it is more acceptable than that employed by the Hanafi school.[106] The only point which should be added to the majority view is that in this case *taghrib*, like *nafi* in *hiraba*, can be imprisonment and not necessarily banishment, as the word literally implies.[107]

However, the distinction between *"muhsan"* and *"ghair-muhsan,"* expressed in English by the terms "adulterer" and "fornicator," is based on the fact that a married person has no reason to commit *zina* since he or she can enjoy lawful sexual relations with his or her spouse. This is an opportunity not available to the unmarried; consequently, the punishment of the unmarried should be lighter than that of the married.[108]

In short, the punishment for *zina*, like all other punishments, is based on moral principles, and since it cannot be claimed that the immorality of this act when committed by a unmarried person is the same as when committed by the married, the punishment differs in each case.[109]

This distinction can be rationally understood. One cannot understand, however, how the status of *ihsan* could be considered to continue in case of the dissolution of the marriage. If the reason behind imposing a severe punishment upon a married person is that he or she can have lawful sexual relations with his or her spouse, this condition of *ihsan* should be considered to exist if, and only if, the culprit has committed adultery during a valid marriage. But if the reason behind this punishment is that the person has had lawful sexual relations at one time, then what was said about the continuity of the status of *ihsan* could be correct but still difficult to understand.[110]

However, it is reported that the well-known Egyptian jurist and reformer, Muhammad 'Abduh, held that the punishment prescribed by the Prophetic words and practice for the *muhsan* adulterer is only applicable in cases of offenders who, at the time of committing the offence, were parties to a valid marital relationship. According to 'Abduh, the punishment of the offender who has been married, but is no longer so, should be lighter or at most equal to that of the unmarried offender.[111]

In conclusion, it is worth quoting the view of a contemporary scholar, Professor Shalabi, on the question of punishment of adultery. In accordance with the above-mentioned requirement of proof, Shalabi states, "This punishment is prescribed in fact for those who committed the crime openly . . . with no consideration for the law or for the feeling of the community. . . ."[112] Without doubt, the commission of the crime in this way justifies the punishment prescribed for it.

VI. False Accusations of Unchastity *(al-Qadhf)*

The fourth crime for which the *hadd* punishment is prescribed in the Qur'an is known as *qadhf*. This offence may be defined as an unproved allegation that an individual has committed *zina*.[113] The accused should be *muhsan*. However, in this case *ihsan* has a different meaning than it does when used in connection with *zina;* in this context it means chaste.[114] Jurists of the Sunni schools hold that in order to consider such an assertion an offence, the accused must be a sane adult Muslim who is known to be a chaste person. In my opinion, the preferable view is that of the Zahiris as expressed by Ibn Hazm in *Al-Muhalla*.[115] This view can be summarized by stating that since *ihsan* in its above meaning is the only condition set by the Qur'an, it is likewise the only condition to be required on the part of the accused. At the same time, there is nothing to support the views of the other schools in requiring additional conditions.[116]

The punishment for such slander *(qadhf)* is prescribed in Surah XXIV, verses 4–5: "And those who accuse honourable women but do not bring four witnesses, flog them (with) eighty stripes and never (again) accept their testimony. They are indeed evil-doers, except those who afterwards repent and make amends." It is controversial whether or not these verses were revealed because of the false accusation against 'Aisha, the Prophet's wife, an incident mentioned in verses 11–22 of the same surah.[117]

According to those who hold that this punishment was prescribed because of the incident involving 'Aisha, the punishment has a retroactive force, while according to others, who maintain that the verses concerned were revealed before this incident, the punishment does not have this force.[118] However, it is a fact that the first instance in which this punishment was inflicted was that relating to 'Aisha.[119] Three people, namely, Hassan b. Thabit, Mistah b. Athatha, and Himna b. Jahsh were punished accordingly.[120]

The jurists differ in regard to some aspects of the problems raised concerning the punishment for *qadhf*. In this study we will limit our discussion to three controversial points: (1) the question of whether the accusation must be clear or whether it can be mere insinuation; (2) the categorization of the punishment into *haqq adami* or *haqq Allah*; and (3) the effect of the criminal's repentance.

But before beginning the discussion of these points, it should be stated that the punishment for this crime is not an exception to the rule that a crime should not draw more than one punishment. As for *qadhf*, the previously cited Qur'anic verses prescribe three punishments, two of which are to be carried out in this world, i.e., eighty lashes and rejection of the criminal's testimony,[121] while the third involves the culprit's relationship with his Creator, that is, he will be considered a sinner. These two punishments are our main concern in this study. As a matter of fact, the rejection of the offender's testimony is a relatively incidental one when compared to the principal punishment, the eighty lashes.

VI. 1. The Clarity or Insinuativeness of the Accusation

A clear accusation is one which is expressed in a word which does not have more than one meaning, that is, a word derived from the word *zina* or any word having the same meaning. On the other hand, an insinuated accusation is one in which the accuser uses a word which merely means, among other things, that the accused has committed the crime of *zina*.

Except for the Maliki school, all jurists agree that there can be no *hadd* punishment unless the accuser has used an unambiguous word.[122] The Maliki school, on the other hand, holds that the insinuated accusation does not differ from one which is clear insofar as the accused is able to understand that the accuser was implying *zina* and was accusing him of having committed it.[123] The problem here is of a linguistic nature in which it is to be determined whether an insinuation can be considered, linguistically, a clear expression or not. As far as the Arabic language is concerned, the Qur'an is considered the highest authority for solving problems of Arabic usage. The Qur'an contains many verses which distinguish between insinuation or intimation and clarity.[124] Hence one can say that the majority view on this matter is the preferable one.

At the same time, when someone uses a word which has several meanings, one of which can be understood as *zina*, he may be liable to a *ta'zir* punishment when the *hadd* punishment is not to be applied.[125]

VI. 2. The Categorization of the Punishment

There are three views among the jurists concerning the categorization of the punishment for *qadhf*. The Hanafi and Zahiri schools agree in that this punishment pertains to the public sphere, or, to use a modern expression, it is a state punishment because the punishment is designed to safeguard the public interest by protecting the individual's reputation. Thus, it pertains to that part of the criminal law known in Islamic terminology as *haqq Allah*.[126]

According to the Shafi'i and Hanbali schools, the punishment for *qadhf* is *haqq adami*. Hence, it cannot be imposed unless the accused or his representative demand it; if he forgives his accuser there is no punishment.[127]

The Maliki jurists make a distinction between the case before and after it is brought before the judge. Before the case is reported to the judge, it falls in the category of *haqq adami,* and afterwards it becomes *haqq Allah*.[128] This distinction is in fact applicable to all the *hadd* punishments; in several *ahadith* the Prophet recommends forgiving wrong-doers before their crimes are reported to the judge. However, once the crime has been reported, the punishment, if proved, must be carried out.[129] In any case, this recommendation has nothing to do with the categorization of the punishment; hence, its application by the Maliki school to this particular situation cannot be accepted.

Although Hanafi scholars hold the view that this punishment pertains to *haqq Allah*, they are of the opinion that the punishment should not be inflicted unless requested by the accused or his representative.[130] To justify this view, the relevant Qur'anic verses and *ahadith* should be studied. Neither in the Qur'an nor in the Sunna is there any proof that the imposition of this punishment should depend on the request of the accused. It is clear that when the Prophet imposed the punishment for *qadhf* upon those who were guilty of it in respect to 'Aisha,[131] he did not ask her if she wanted it to be inflicted upon her accusers.[132] Consequently, since this condition cannot be sustained by proofs, the Zahiri view remains the preferable one.

On the other hand, the Hanbali and Shafi'i schools, in support of their view that this punishment belongs to the category of *haqq adami*, emphasize the agreement that they claim to have existed concerning the condition of the accused's request for punishment. However, since this condition is no longer accepted, their view also should not be approved.[133]

To sum up, the punishment for *qadhf* is one which pertains to the realm of the public interest, *haqq Allah*. The infliction of this punishment is not dependent upon the request of the accused, and once the crime is proved either by testimony or by confession, the guilty person should be punished. The principle of forgiveness before the matter is reported to the judge still applies to the crime of *qadhf* but without affecting the fact that its punishment is classified as *haqq Allah*.[134]

VI. 3. The Effect of the Criminal's Repentance

It has already been mentioned that the Qur'anic verses relating to *qadhf* specify "except those who afterwards repent . . ."(XXIV:5). The effect of this repentance is, however, controversial.

According to the Hanafi school, this repentance does not affect the fact that the criminal's future testimony is to be rejected.[135] The Shafi'i, Maliki, Hanbali, and Zaydi schools hold a contrary view, according to which the testimony of the criminal can be accepted after his repentance.[136]

The controversy on this matter stems from the jurists' differing interpretations of the last part of the above-mentioned Qur'anic verse. Those who believe that the exception, "except those who afterwards repent . . .," applies only to the sentence before it, "they indeed are evil-doers," hold that the criminal's repentance does not affect the requirement that his testimony should be rejected; this view is held by the Hanafi jurists. On the other hand, the jurists who hold that this exception applies to the entire verse preceding it maintain the opposite opinion.[137] All jurists, however, agree that although this exception does not affect the *hadd* punishment, it does affect the verdict in the sense of considering the criminal as an "evil-doer."[138] This concludes our discussion of the *hadd* punishments, but the topic still needs to be surveyed in order to explain its underlying philosophy.

VII. A Survey of *Hadd* Punishments

The *hadd* punishments in Islamic law were prescribed by God in the Qur'an, with the exception of one offence, adultery (or *zina* committed by a married person), for which the punishment is prescribed in the Sunna of the Prophet.

Very little has been said about the nature and purpose of this aspect of Islamic criminal law. The Muslim jurists were not interested in discussing the matter as they saw these punishments as the province of God alone. Since they have been prescribed in specific terms and are to be imposed without question, it was considered unnecessary to say much about the purposes they served or the reasons for which they were prescribed.

To the best of my knowledge, the first Muslim jurist who dealt with these aspects of the *hadd* was Ibn al-Qayyim. We find them discussed in his book *I'lam al-Muwaqq'in* and in other works.[139] Unfortunately, after him the subject returned to its former oblivion. It was not until comparatively recently that some Muslim jurists turned their attention to it and wrote several works concerning it.[140] All that has been written in this connection is far from being comparable to Western penology, for on the whole it tends to be little more than an explanation of one aspect or another of Islamic criminal law. For this reason, a survey of the *hadd* punishments is not an easy undertaking, especially when one attempts to compare it with Western thought.

In Western penology it is almost universally accepted that punishment has three principal purposes: retribution, deterrence, and reformation, although the demarcations among these are not always clear, and sub-classifications may be necessary.[141]

The belief in the importance of retribution is universal. In England, not only is the public usually adamant in demanding retributive punishment for the offender, but the doctrine also has a well-established place in British jurisprudence and philosophy; even religious teachers give it their support.[142] As Goodhart stated, "Retribution in punishment is an expression of the community's disapproval of crime, and if this retribution is not given recognition, then the disapproval may also disappear. A community which is too ready to forgive the wrongdoer may end by condoning crime."[143]

Very recently the retributive theory of punishment has been the subject of considerable debate. The ideas of the eighteenth century philosopher Immanuel Kant have been given more attention than any other formulations of retributive theories.[144] Kant's theory may be summarized in this sentence: ". . . Punishment can never be administered merely as a means for promoting another Good, either with regard to the criminal himself, or to civil society, but must in all cases be imposed only because the individual on whom it is inflicted has committed a crime."[145] This theory has, however, suffered from various misinterpretations, none of which will be discussed here. The most sensible interpretation is that offered by John Rawls and illustrated by Ted Honderich.[146] They hold that retributionists do not advocate, as an institution, "legal machinery whose essential purpose is to set up and preserve a correspondence between moral turpitude and suffering.'' But they rightly insist "that no man can be punished unless he is guilty, that is, unless he has broken the law.''[147]

It will serve no purpose in this study to discuss the strengths and weaknesses of this theory. Our main concern here is to call attention to the justification given to it in legal and philosophical writings in order to illustrate its application in the Islamic penal system. It may be said, in summary, that "the consequences of punishment, other than the immediate deprivation suffered by the criminals, are irrelevant to its justification.''[148]

Finally, retribution has much in common with the motive of expiation, so much so that it is often confused with it. Both retribution and expiation are concerned with rooting out the criminal's evil. The retributive element in punishment means that sanctions have been imposed on the criminal for his wrongdoing; expiation, on the other hand, means that the criminal has "paid" for his crime and that his account with society is now clear.[149]

VII.   1.   Retribution and *Hadd* Punishments

The retributive function of *hadd* punishment is the one most commonly discussed by Muslim jurists, in addition to its deterrent function, to which we will shortly refer. Retribution is mentioned in the Qur'an as the purpose of punishment in many verses referring to punishment both in this world and in the Hereafter.[150] It is interesting to note that the Arabic word for retribution, *jaza*, in Qur'anic usage means both punishment and reward.[151] This indicates that both punishment and reward are used as means for the same end, an approach which may be compared with a similar function of punishment and reward in modern philosophy.[152]

In the Islamic penal system two points should be noted in respect to retribution as a feature of the *hadd* punishments: the severity of the punishment, and the prohibition of any mediation in respect to it; in other words, its mandatory infliction when the crime has been proved.

The penalties prescribed in Islamic law for the crimes of *hudud* are the most severe punishments known to mankind for such crimes. Still more severe punishments, however, were prescribed in English law, during the eighteenth and nineteenth centuries, for example, although today they no longer exist.[153] The punishments prescribed in Islamic law, on the other hand, which are still accepted by hundreds of millions of people, are implemented in some countries such as Saudi Arabia, and, what is more, the demand for their application in other Muslim countries becomes stronger from time to time.[154] According to Muhammad Qutb, the severity of the punishment is based on psychological considerations. In order to combat the criminal's inclination to break the law, Islam prescribed severe punishments which draw attention to the consequences of the crime, acting as a deterrent to its commission.[155] The same explanation is given by 'Uda in his book on Islamic criminal legislation.[156]

However, severity of punishment is a controversial point. On the one hand, some philosophers hold that "treatment" rather than punishment is what the criminal needs;[157] on the other, some judges demand the reintroduction of severer penalties, including corporal punishment, in Western countries as the only means of controlling the increasing crime rate.[158] No matter what view one holds on this point, there is no doubt that retributive punishment can be nothing but severe. It is for this reason, I think, that the Muslim jurists justify the *hadd* punishments in terms of retributive penalties.[159]

Nevertheless, the degree of severity is not and cannot be agreed upon.[160] Muslim jurists justify the severity of the *hadd* punishments because they are prescribed by God; consequently, they cannot be objected to and are eternally to be considered the most suitable punishments for the crimes for which they are prescribed.[161] To emphasize the fact that God created people, defined what is right and what is wrong for them, and determined the suitable punishments for wrong-doing, they quote the Qur'anic verse, "Should He not know what He created? And He is the Subtle, the Aware" (XLVII:14). Hence, to try to justify the *hadd* punishments in secular or, in other words, modern terms would take us beyond the scope of this study and might fail to achieve any meaningful consensus.

The second aspect in which *hadd* punishments seem to be retributive is the obligatory nature of their execution once the crime has been proved. In a well-known *hadith,* the Prophet prohibited any mediation in carrying out the *hadd* punishments and indicated that even if his daughter Fatimah had committed a *hadd* crime, he would impose punishment on her like anyone else.[162]

I interpret this prohibition of mediation or the requirement of obligatory implementation of the punishment as a retributive feature in *hadd* punishment. In other words, if mediation were allowed or if the *hadd* punishments could be replaced by any other punishments, their retributive effect would no longer exist. Hence, it may be said that the severity of the punishment and the requirement that it must be carried out, combine to give the punishment as full a retributive effect as possible.

Thus far only the role of retributive theory in relation to the general rules regarding *hadd* punishments has been discussed. But its clearer and more important influence appears in the approaches and views of jurists concerning some more detailed aspects. One of these relates to the question of imposing cumulative sentences on one offender (*ta'adud al-'uqubat*). Sentences may be cumulative when the same person has committed various offences before he stands trial or before being punished for any one of them. The offences committed by the same individual may either be of the same kind, e.g., theft, highway robbery, and housebreaking, or of a different kind, e.g., theft, adultery, and drinking alcohol. In the first case it is agreed that the offender deserves one punishment for all his offences,[163] while in the second case such agreement is lacking. Three schools, the Hanafi, Maliki, and Hanbali hold one position on this matter, while the Shafi'i school takes a different view. With its non-recognition of the practice of abrogation (*jabb*), to which we will return later, the Shafi'i school understands the primary role of retributive theory in this context, maintaining that the offender deserves as many sentences as his offences. All the sentences earned are to be carried out, starting with those imposed for offences classified as *haqq adami*.

If, however, the offender has been sentenced to death for homicide (which likewise is *haqq adami*), then this sentence is to be carried out last; that is, the death penalty should be the last punishment, disregarding the classification of the offence for which it has been imposed.[164] To explain this view, the Shafi'i scholars give the hypothetical example of an unmarried man who makes an unproven accusation of fornication and who committs *zina*, theft, armed robbery, and homicide (for which two latter charges he has been sentenced to death). In this case, they say, the punishments are to be imposed starting with the lightest. Thus, the offender should be punished first for the unproved accusation of fornication, second for *zina*, third for theft, and then he is to be executed for homicide, his execution covering the crime of armed robbery as well.[165]

The Shafi'is' view reflects their strong belief in retribution as the philosophy underlying the concept of *hadd* punishment. Their view is an application of the principle of *jus talionis* as explained by the retributionists, that is, "A man must be punished if he has performed an act for which he deserves a penalty. Further, he must not be given a lesser penalty than he deserves for his action."[166]

The retributive theory also predominates in the Shafi'i and Hanbali positions relating to punishing an insane man whose guilt has been established by testimony. The assumption is, of course, that the offender has committed the offence while in full possession of his faculties and that he was sane when tried and sentenced. The onset of his insanity was after the pronouncement of the sentence but prior to its implementation. The Shafi'is and Hanbalis hold that in such a case the offender should be punished because he committed the offence while sane and therefore responsible for his actions.[167]

It is a unanimously held view that a sentence pronounced against a pregnant woman should be suspended until she has given birth to her child and recovered from her confinement.[168] This view is based on the fact that the authority does not have the right to inflict harm on the child by punishing his mother, for while the mother deserves punishment, the child is innocent.[169] This rule of limiting the effect of punishment to the person who has earned it is well-established in the retributive doctrine.[170]

VII. 2   The Concept of Expiation

It has been said that retribution is often confused with expiation. The expiatory view reflects the belief "that in suffering his punishment the offender has purged his guilt, has 'paid for' his crime, and that his account with society is therefore clear. This is the attitude for example which lies behind the commonly expressed reluctance to hold a man's record against him after his discharge from prison."[171] The concept of expiation in Islamic law however has a different aim. Its purpose is not to clear the person's account with society but with God. The Arabic word for expiation is *kaffara*, which is mentioned in the Qur'an in relation to such matters as accidental homicide, swearing a false oath, and failing to observe religious duties during the *hajj* or pilgrimage. But these cases, except for that of accidental homicide, are clearly not connected with the penal system of Islam; rather, they are all concerned with man's relationship to his Creator. Even in the context of the *hadd* punishments, when expiation is mentioned, it refers to man's relationship with God and not with his fellow citizens or society. It is narrated that the Prophet said

"Whoever commits a crime deserving of *hadd* and receives its punishment, this will be its expiation;"[172] that is to say, the offender who has been punished in this world will not be punished in the Hereafter. Thus it is obvious that the concept of expiation in Islam differs completely from the legal concept of expiation known in Western law, for it is one which is essentially religious and which cannot be considered as part of the theory of punishment in its legal context.

VII. 3. Deterrence and *Hadd* Punishments

According to Professor Blanshard, "Whatever else it may be, punishment is commonly supposed to be a deterrent of crime."[173] Deterrence is often characterized as a justification for punishment which looks to the future, i.e., to the prevention of crime. In this respect it is in contrast to the theory of retribution, which is often said to be a justification for punishment which looks to the past, i.e., to the offence as an event isolated from possible future events. Retributionists, however, may argue that their theory does not hold that an individual's punishment is wholly justified by an event in the past. "It includes the contention that a man's punishment provides satisfaction" to the victim of his offence and to others. This satisfaction, in the deterrence theory, is "of relatively small importance. What is taken to be of supreme importance is that punishment prevents offences."[174]

The deterrent effect is known to have a dual impact. There is the general deterrent, i.e., the preventive effect of a penal system (or a particular aspect of it) on criminality in the population at large, as well as the particular deterrent, i.e., the inhibitive effect of the punishment of an individual.[175] General deterrence is achieved by giving the actual punishment, when it is inflicted, the widest possible publicity; individual deterrence comes into play when an offender suffers the penalty.[176] Individual deterrence involves making the offender reluctant to offend again, rendering it difficult to distinguish it from reformation which is supposed to achieve the same end. In some theories, a line is drawn between moral improvement or reformation which induce the offender to repudiate crime on moral grounds, and prevention which merely frightens him off. But others regard this frightening-off process as coming under the heading of deterrence.[177]

Be that as it may, this is one instance of the lack of clarity of the boundary lines between the different theories of punishment, and it is this question of the frightening-off of the individual as a means of protecting society from crimes which raises the major criticism against deterrence. Howard Jones points out that the aim of deterrent punishment is to instil in the individual a respect for the law based on his fear of the punishment which will follow if he transgresses. He also raised the critical question of "whether legally correct behaviour maintained for such reasons is worth having." To pose the question in such a way, Jones continues, "seems to me to be very naive." The element of fear "does already enter to a very considerable extent into the social training of all of us."[178] This point was emphasized by Archbishop Temple when he said that "this fear in no way derogates from the value of the sentiments we afterwards build on these foundations. They may begin as rationalizations for our real motives of fear, but they develop into sincerely held moral principles, to which, when they are matured, we cling in the face of the most appalling temptations and difficulties."[179]

However, this is only one objection to the deterrent theory; philosophers often are engaged in putting forward and replying to many other objections. Although it may be interesting to participate in some of these arguments, my inclination here is to conclude that, in spite of all the objections against the deterrence theory, it is still widely recognized as a valid justification for punishment.[180]

The recognition of the deterrence aspect in the Islamic penal system is deeper and stronger than in other systems. Here deterrence is recognized as the predominant justification for punishments, particularly for *hadd* punishments. Mawardi, certainly influenced by the place given to the deterrence theory in Islamic legal works, defined the *hudud* as "deterrent punishments which God established to prevent man from committing what He forbade and from neglecting what He commanded."[181] If, as it was argued,[182] deterrence is to be achieved by means of severe punishments, then we need not say much about the deterrence theory as the justification of punishment in Islamic law. But the fact is that punishment is justified because, according to the deterrence theory, it prevents the commission of further offences, both by the offender and by other members of the society. The dual notions of general and special deterrence are known to Muslim jurists and supported as one of the basic motivations behind the *hadd* punishments.[183]

The most common example given by contemporary Muslim writers as evidence of the deterrent effect of the *hadd* punishments is the enormous decrease in the crime rate in Saudi Arabia since their re-introduction in that country. During the Ottoman administration of the Arabian Peninsula, the *hadd* punishments were not applied. In the late 1920's, when the Saudis took over, they reintroduced them, ordering judges to implement the teachings of the Hanbali school in entirety, including those relating to penal law. Soon after this order, the crime rate fell noticeably.[184] It is said, for example, that official figures indicate that the *hadd* punishment for theft has never been carried out in Saudi Arabia more than twice a year.[185] This was stressed in the Arab Conference on Crime and Treatment of Offenders held in Kuwait in 1970.[186]

In this context it is interesting to note that a punishment similar to that prescribed in the Qur'an for theft has halted all types of theft in the Irish province of Ardoyne (Belfast). This was administered by the I.R.A. and reported, understandably, as "Rough Justice" in *The Times*.[187] Moreover, and rather astonishingly, an American philosopher stated that "touching a hot stove and getting once painfully burned causes one automatically to refrain from touching a hot stove again. So, if pick-pockets were similarly painfully burned or cut by the purse they reach for, they would similarly stop picking pockets."[188] It is the need for deterrent punishments and the belief in the validity of the deterrence theory which underlies both the American philosopher's view and the experience of the Irish Republican Army. The success of the Saudi Arabian experience is also frequently cited as evidence of the effectiveness of *hadd* punishments.

Leaving aside the practical aspects, the jurists of all schools of Islamic law have laid great stress on the deterrence theory. According to Ibn al-Humam, the well-known Hanafi jurist, the *hadd* punishments are prescribed as general deterrents; but when an individual experiences punishment for one of the *hadd* offences, the aspect of individual deterrence comes into play.[189] The same view is expressed by many of the commentators on the Qur'an.[190] It is also agreed that all *hadd* punishments should be carried out in public in order to achieve the fullest deterrent effect. Because the Qur'an commands that the punishment for adultery be carried out in public, the jurists extended this command to all other *hadd* punishments.[191] This, as mentioned above, is a clear application of the deterrence theory.

However, the views expressed by the jurists on certain aspects of the question may give a clearer illustration of the issues involved. Here we shall deal with two aspects in some detail, i.e., disinheritance as an incidental punishment for homicide and the rejection of the offender's testimony as an incidental punishment for a slanderous accusation regarding chastity and other *hadd* offences.

VII. 3. 1. Disinheritance and Deprivation of Legacy

In cases of deliberate homicide, and apart from the punishment of retaliation *(qisas)* or the payment of blood-money *(diya)*, if the murderer happens to be an heir of the victim, or if the victim has appointed the murderer as his legatee, the murderer can be deprived of his right as an heir or legatee. This rule of deprivation is known as *al-hirman min al-mirath wal-wasiyah*. It is based on a *hadith* narrated in several different ways *(turuq)*, the most trustworthy of which states, "Nothing will be given to the murderer."[192] All the schools of Islamic law agree on the application of this rule; however, each school or group of schools has its own view as to how it is to be interpreted.[193]

The Hanafi, Shafi'i, Hanbali, and Zaydi schools apply this rule to both deliberate and accidental homicide.[194] This view is based first on the generality *('umum)* of the words of the relevant *ahadith*, and, secondly, on the accepted rule of *usul al-fiqh* known as the prevention of excuses *(sadd al-dharaic)*. That is to say, if a person were allowed the right to inherit from the victim he accidentally killed, it would encourage every such murderer to claim that he had committed accidental homicide. It is therefore better to avoid this issue altogether by applying the rule of deprivation to all cases of homicide.[195]

The jurists of the Maliki school hold that only deliberate murder should be considered as a bar to inheritance. Neither accidental homicide nor deliberate but lawful homicide (as in carrying out a punishment or in self-defense) affect inheritance.[196] This approach views disinheritance as a punishment which may be inflicted only for a wrong done or for a crime committed. The Maliki jurists maintain that the reason for the deprivation of inheritance is that the murderer had tried, or is assumed to have tried, to get his portion of the inheritance before the due time, while this is not the case in either accidental or lawful murder.[197]

As for the deprivation of legacy, the schools of Islamic law hold three differing views. The Hanafi, Zaydi, Hanbali, and some of the Shafi' scholars maintain that since the nature of legacy is the same as inheritance, the same rule of deprivation should be applied by way of analogy *(qiyas)*. The rest of the Shafi'i scholars and the jurists of the Maliki school hold that homicide, even of a deliberate kind, is not a proper reason for the deprivation of a legacy.[199] In other words, they restrict the application of the above-mentioned *hadith* to inheritance, while the holders of the opposite view extend it to cover a legacy as well. The third view is held by some scholars who differentiate between two assumptions regarding a legacy. The first is that the murdered person had made his will before his death, or before the action which led to his death. In this case they deprive the murderer of his right to the legacy. In the second case, they assume that after the act which resulted in his death, the victim bequeathed some of his property to his murderer. Here they grant the murderer the right to take the money on the grounds that the principle behind the rule of deprivation, namely, that the murderer had tried to take possession of his heritage before the due time, is inapplicable.[200]

The rule that murder is a bar to inheritance and legacy is to be interpreted in the light of the fact that the Islamic penal system is generally based on the concept of deterrence. It is true that homicide is not a *hadd* offence, but this does not affect the validity of this example. In Islamic law homicide is regarded, as we shall see in due course, as a private wrong or a tort rather than a public wrong or a crime. Under Islamic law the murderer may be punished by the death penalty or by paying blood-money *(diya)*; the choice lies in the hands of the victim's relatives who may even pardon the offender altogether. This approach to the treatment of homicide led the jurists to make good use of the above-mentioned *hadith*. As we have stated above, some jurists apply it even to cases of accidental homicide, in which there was no criminal intent whatsoever. This cannot be understood unless it is related to the jurists' aim of deterring people from committing the offence.[201]

VII. 3. 2. Rejection of the Offender's Testimony

In dealing with the punishment for *qadhf*, it was mentioned that this offence in fact entailes two punishments: flogging and the rejection of the offender's testimony. Here we are not concerned with every minute detail discussed by the jurists. However, more may be said later about the qualifications of witnesses. The most fundamental condition is that a witness should possess "a quality of high moral integrity which is known as *'adala.''*[202] Jurists classify those convicted of a *hadd* offence and punished for it as lacking this qualification, and consequently as unfit to give evidence before the court.[203] Generally it is held that this rejection of testimony should come to an end as soon as the offender repents.[204] This rule of rejection has no basis in the Qur'an or in the Sunna except in cases of *qadhf*. For other *hadd* offences, the jurists apply it on the grounds that the offender has lost his "moral integrity" or *'adala*. Such restrictions are also to be interpreted as a means of deterring people from committing the offences in question. Since the person who is not *'adl* would not be considered as reliable, no one, at least no one who is concerned with his good repute, would risk losing it. This is the only explanation one can give for extending the rule of rejection of testimony to all the *hadd* offences, despite its Qur'anic restriction to the offence of *qadhf*.

It may be suggested that disqualification is not in fact grounded in the deterrent theory. It could simply be based on the unreliability of the offender in that after committing a *hadd* offence, he can no longer be believed. But when we realize that in a Muslim society the rejection of an individual's testimony is tantamount to outlawing him, the view that the rejection of the testimony of one who has committed a *hadd* offence is a deterrent measure finds support.

VII.   4.   Reformation and *Hadd* Punishments

Due to extensive research on the subject of crime and punishment during the last hundred years, reformation has come to be seen as one of the major results which punishment is supposed to achieve.[205] For some criminologists "reformation" is rapidly becoming synonymous with "cure." The criminal is no longer a "bad man" but a "sick man."[206] The belief in the need for reformative punishment appears to have reached its peak in the last ten years, leading some thinkers to argue that "a convict needs treatment. He is genuinely ill, perhaps physically, almost certainly mentally, and psychiatrically. He is truly a sick man. He needs help. Something has gone wrong which leads him to react in an antisocial way in situations which stimulate others to constructive actions."[207]

The increased emphasis on reformation has had a very considerable effect on the types of punishment employed and on the penal systems in nearly all Western countries.[208] On the other hand, the reformative theory is still being criticized, and the controversy continues. It should be said, however, that modern criminologists are generally against the theory that crime is the result of illness.[209]

Whatever be the place of the reformative theory in Western penology, it has no place in the justification of the *hadd* punishments of Islamic law, because these punishments are based on what God has decreed. He alone has prescribed these punishments for the stated crimes, and whether or not they will reform the offender, in the sense of equating reform with treatment, is not relevant to the discussion.[210]

In spite of this fact, however, Ibn al-Qayyim claimed that the *hadd* punishments are of reformative as well as retributive and deterrent value.[211] He explained this value by referring to the fact, which is well-established among the Muslim jurists, that an individual who has received his punishment in this world will not be punished for it in the Hereafter.[212] But his explanation, although supported by some *ahadith* reported to have been narrated by some of the Prophet's Companions and in harmony with the divine nature of Islamic law, does not, from a penologist's point of view, imply that the *hadd* punishments have a reformative element in the sense in which the word "reform" is understood in legal writing. Consequently, the *hadd* punishments are only of retributive and deterrent value as we have seen earlier.

This view, however, has one exception, that is, in regard to the fourth aspect of the *hadd* punishment for *hiraba*, i.e., *nafi*. As we have seen, the offender who has been sentenced to this punishment is to be exiled or imprisoned until he displays good behavior and does not seem likely to commit another crime. This sort of punishment is clearly prescirbed to improve the criminal's character. Hence, in this case one can say that it is aimed at reformation, and it stands as the sole exception to the general theory of *hadd* punishments.

NOTES

1. The Arabic word *hudud* (s. *hadd*) has many different meanings. The limit of something, e.g., a place or a piece of land, is its *hadd*. The man who carries out the punishment is called *haddad*, which derives from the same root. See Subki and 'Abd al-Hamid, *Mukhtar al-Sihah*, p. 94, and Ibn Hajar, *Fath al-Bari*, vol. XII, pp. 47-48.
2. Qarafi, *Furuq*, vol. I, pp. 140-142.

3. Kasani, *Badai'*, vol. VII, pp. 33–56; 'Uda, *Al-Tashri' al-Jina'i al-Islami*, vol. I, p. 79; Abu Zahra, *Al-Jarimah*, p. 56.
4. Qur'an, Surah II, verse 229. See Ibn Taymiyya, *Al-Siyasa'al-Shar'iya'*, pp. 69–70 125.
5. See what follows concerning the punishment for theft.
6. Ibn Hajar, op. cit., p. 47; Ibn Taymiyya, op. cit., pp. 66–126; Shu'rani, *Mizan*, vol. II, p. 134.
7. Unless otherwise stated, the translations of the Qur'anic verses quoted in this work are from M. M. Pickthall, with some modifications.
8. Bukhari, vol. 12, p. 90; Muslim, vol. V, pp. 114-115.
9. Ibn Taymiyya, *op.cit.*, pp. 69-70, 125.
10. Kasani, *Badai'*, vol. VII, p. 65; Ibn al-Humam, vol. IV, p. 218; Siyaghi, *Al-Rawd al-Nadir*, vol. IV, p. 511; Ibn Qudama, *Al-Mughni*, vol. IX, p. 104.
11. Kasani, *Badai'*, vol. VII, p. 77; Ibn 'Abdin, *Al-Haishya*, vol. V, p. 83; Ibn al Humam, op.cit., p. 221.
12. Malik b. Anas, *Al-Muwatta'*, p. 519.
13. Ibid., pp. 327, 520.
14. *Al-Mughni*, vol. VIII, pp. 242–244; Abu Ya'la, *Al-Ahkam al-Sultaniya*, p. 250 'Uda, *Al-Tashri' al-Jina'i al-Islami*, vol. II, pp. 581–582.
15. Shafi'i, *Al-Umm*, vol. VI, p. 134.
16. Siyaghi, op.cit., vol. IV, p. 514.
17. Ibn Hazm, *Al-Muhalla*, vol. XI, p. 352.
18. Ibid., p. 353.
19. Ibid., p. 352.
20. A decision or verdict based on *maslaha* is one which provides the best solution for particular problem in order to meet the community's needs and protect its interests Some of the Qur'anic and Prophetic verdicts are of this kind, as well as a great de. of the jurists' reasoning. See n. 21 below.
21. Shalabi, *Al-Fiqh al-Islami Bayn al-Mithaliya wal-Waqi'ya*, pp. 110–117, 165–17? For details, see his book, *Ta'lil al-Ahkam*, especially pp. 307–322; al-Shatibi, *A. Muwafaqat*, vol. IV, p. 149 ff.
22. Al-Shatibi, op.cit., throughout many pages of this four-volume work; Shalab op.cit., throughout the study.
23. *I'lam al-Muwaqqi'in*, vol. II, p. 64.
24. Shu'rani, op.cit., vol. II, p. 142.
25. Kasani, op.cit., vol. VII, p. 86; Shu'rani, op.cit.
26. For the views of the Maliki school, see Ibn Juza'iy, *Qwanin*, p. 390. For b. Hanb see Ibn Qudama, *Al-Mughni*, vol. VIII, p. 264. For Shafi'i see al-Muzan *Mukhtasar al-Umm*, published on the margin of *Al-Umm*, *Kitab al-Sha'b*, vol. V p. 171.
27. *Al-Muhalla*, vol. XI, pp. 356–357.
28. For the Zaydi school, see al-Siyaghi, op.cit., p. 524; see also *Mughni*, pp. 25 264.
29. *Al-Muhalla*, pp. 334–335; Siyaghi, op.cit., p. 525.
30. XIX:64.
31. Shalabi, op.cit., p. 207.
32. *Al-Muhalla*, p. 357.
33. For the application of this rule with regard to theft, see 'Amer, A., *Al-Ta'zir Shari'a al-Islamiya*, pp. 154–195.
34. Ibn Juza'iy, op. cit., p. 390; cf. Shu'rani, op.cit., p. 142.

35. For a more detailed discussion, see *Al-Muhalla*, pp. 357–358, and Siyaghi, op.cit., pp. 525–526.
36. Ibn al-Humam, op.cit., p. 238; Malik, op.cit., p. 519; Shafi'i, *Umm*, vol. VI, pp. 135–136; *Mughni*, vol. VIII, p. 248; Siyaghi, op.cit., pp. 516–522.
37. *Muhalla*, vol. XI, pp. 319–327.
38. Tabrizi, *Mishkat al-Masabih*, with the commentary of Albani, vol. II, pp. 297, 301.
39. *Umm*, pp. 135–136; Ibn Juza'iy, op.cit., p. 389; *Mughni*, pp. 248–249. For the changeability of rules based on custom in Islamic law, see a scholarly chapter in Shalabi, *Al-Fiqh al-Islami*, pp. 61–94.
40. Sarakhsi, *Al-Mabusut*, vol. IX, p. 195: Tannukhi, *Al-Mudawwanah*, vol. XV, p. 98; Ibn Rushd, *Bidayat al-Mujtahid*, vol. II, p. 493; Ibn 'Abdin, op.cit., vol. IV, p. 113.
41. Tannukhi, *Al-Mudawwanah;* 'Uda, *Al-Tashri' al-Jina'i al-Islami*, vol. II, P. 638.
42. Kasani, op. cit., vol. VII, p. 90; Mawardi, *Al-Ahkam al-Sultaniya*, p. 62.
43. Bukhari, op.cit., vol. XII, pp. 91–94; Muslim, op. cit., vol. V, pp. 101–102.
44. For this view, see al-Tabari, *Tafsir*, vol. VI, p. 119, and against it, Ibn Hazm, *Al-Muhalla*, vol. XI, pp. 310–312. See also 'Uda, op. cit. vol. I, pp. 267–268.
45. Ibn Hazm, op. cit.
46. For this view, see 'Uda, op. cit.
47. See Ibn Hajar's commentary on Bukhari, vol. III, p.78; *Umm*, vol. VI, pp. 139–140.
48. The word "village" in Qur'anic or, generally, in Islamic legal terminology does not have the same sense as in common contemporary usage. It denotes an inhabitated place, as distinct from what is called *sahra'* (desert) or an uninhabitated place. See 'Aisha 'Abd al-Rahman, *Al-Qur'an wal-Tafsir al-'Asri*, pp. 51–52.
49. Sarakhsi, *Al-Mabsut*, vol. IX, p. 195 ff.
50. Ibn Rushd, *Bidayat al-Mujtahid*, vol. II, p. 493; Ghazali, *Wajiz*, vol. II, p. 179; *Muhalla*, vol. XI, pp.302–307; Hasani, *Tatimmat al-Rawd al-Nadir*, vol. V, pp. 30–31; Hilli, *Shara'i' al-Islam*, vol. II, p. 257.
51. Mardawi, *Al-Insaf*, vol. X, pp. 291–292.
52. Ghazali, op. cit.; Ramli, *Nihayat al-Muhtaj ila' Sharh al-Minhaj*, a Shafi'i text, vol. VIII, p. 2.
53. Abu Zahra, *Falsafat al-'Uquba*, p. 6.
54. *Umm*, vol. VI, p. 140.
55. ---Missing, they will take care of it.-----
56. *Umm*, vol. VI, p. 140.
57. *Muhalla*, vol. XI, p. 318.
58. See footnotes 22 and 23.
59. For a more detailed discussion, see Shalabi, op. cit., pp. 81–86.
60. Zayla'i, his commentary on *Kanz al-Daqai'q*, vol. III, p. 237. For the view of b. al-Qasim, see *Al-Mudawanab al-Kubra*, vol. XV, p. 99.
61. *Nihayat al-Muhtaj*, p. 5; *Al-Insaf*, vol. X, p. 293; *Bidayat al-Mujtahid*, vol. II, p. 494.
62. *Muhalla*, vol. XI, pp. 317–318.
63. *Al-Mudawwanah*, vol. XV, p. 99.
64. 'Uda, op. cit., vol. I, p. 657.
65. *Muhalla*, vol. XI, p. 317; *Mudawwanah*, vol. XV, pp. 98–105.
66. Qarafi, *Furuq*, vol. III, p. 18.
67. Shafi'i, *Umn*, vol. VI, p. 140; Zayla'i, *Tabyeen al-Haqai'q*, vol. III, pp. 235–237; Mardawi, *Al-Insaf*, p. 292-295.

68.   Qarafi, op. cit.
69.   Zayla'i, op. cit., p. 235.
70.   *Mudawwanah*, vol. XV, pp. 99–100.
71.   Ghazali, *Wajiz*, vol. II, p. 179; Mardawi, *Insaf*, vol. X, p. 298.
72.   See the references mentioned previously, as well as 'Uda, op. cit., vol. I, pp. 660–661.
73.   See sections 59, 60, 61 and 62 of *The Criminal Justice Act of 1967*; for details, see Hall Williams, *The English Penal System in Transition*, pp. 184–190.
74.   'Uda, op. cit., vol. I, pp. 659–660.
75.   See introduction to his book, *Al-Jarima wal-'Uquba*, pp. 6–11.
76.   Mirghinani, *Hidaya*, vol. IV, p. 272; *Ghazali, Wajiz*, p. 179; Ibn Juza'iy, op. cit. p. 392; Mardawi, *Insaf*, vol. X, p. 299.
77.   Kasani, op. cit., vol. VII, p. 33. For other definitions see 'Uda, op. cit., vol. II, p. 349.
78.   *Fath al-Qadir*, vol. V, p. 150; 'Uda, op. cit.
79.   IV:15–16.
80.   Ibn Kathir, *Tafsir al-Qur'an*, vol. I, p. 462; Ibn al-Jawzi, *Zad al-Masir fi 'Ilm al-Tafsir*, vol. II, pp. 33–36; Sayyed Qutb, *Fi Zilal al-Qur'an*, vol. XVIII, pp. 57–58.
81.   Suyuty, *Itqan*, vol. II, p. 23.
82.   Ibn Kathir, op. cit.
83.   See 'Abd al-Qahir al-Baghdadi, *Al-Farq Bayn al-Firaq*, p. 84.
84.   Darwazat, *Al-Dustur al-Qur'ani*, p. 193 ff. The same view was reported by al-Albani in his commentary on *Mukhtasar Sahih Muslim*, vol. II, p. 36, fn. 3, but he did not mention who holds it.
85.   Bukhari, op. cit., vol. XII, pp. 119–124; Suyuty, *Itqan*, vol. II, p. 25; *Muhalla*, vol. XI, pp. 232–237.
86.   Bukhari, op. cit., vol. XII, pp. 101, 108, 115–118; Muslim, op. cit., vol. V, pp. 117, 120–122; *Mishkat al-Masabih*, vol. II, pp. 287–293.
87.   Bukhari, op. cit., pp. 140–145.
88.   This is summarized from Darwazat, op. cit., pp. 193–197.
89.   Bukhari, op. cit., p. 140.
90.   *Ibid.*, p. 120; *Muhalla*, p. 235.
91.   Muslim, vol. V, p. 115.
92.   Ibn Kathir, op. cit., p. 462; *Zad al-Masir*, vol. VI, p. 5, fn. 1.
93.   *Muhalla*, vol. XI, p. 183 ff.; Shu'rani, *Mizan*, vol. II, p. 135 ff.
94.   Mughni, op. cit., vol. VIII, pp. 160 ff., 166 ff.; *Fath al-Qadir*, vol. IV, p. 135 ff.;
95.   Mughni, op. cit.
96.   See *The Jewish Encyclopaedia*, vol. I, under "adultery," and vol. III, under "capital punishment."
97.   For the similarity between the two systems, see Abu-Zahra, *Al-Jarima wal-'Uquba*, pp. 9–10.
98.   Coulson, N.J., *A History of Islamic Law*, p. 83.
99.   *The Jewish Encyclopaedia*, vol. I, p. 217.
100. See below, chapter V, The Law of Evidence in Criminal Cases.
101. For juristic application, see Kasani, *Badai'*, pp. 60–61, and Ibn Farhun, *Tabsirah*, vol. II, p. 183.
102. *Badai' al-Sanai'*, vol. VII, p. 39; Ibn Juzaiy, op. cit., p. 384; *Umm*, vol. VI, p. 119. And for details see *Al-Risalah*, with the commentary of A.M. Shakir, pp. 130 and 245 ff.
103. Mughni, p. 160 ff.; *Muhalla*, vol. XI, p. 234; *Al-Rawd al-Nadir*, vol. IV, p. 481.

104. *Al-Risalah*, pp. 130 and 245 ff.
105. *Al-Risalah and Al-Muhalla*, vol. XI, pp. 181–188 and 232–233.
106. *Badai' al-Sanai'*, vol. VII, p. 39; *Fath al-Qadir*, pp. 134–137.
107. See J. N. D. Anderson, *Islamic Law in Africa*, p. 196, for replacing banishment with imprisonment in Northern Nigeria.
108. See Ibn al-Qayyim, *I'lam al-Muwaqqi'n*, vol. II, p. 107 ff.
109. It is noteworthy that *muhsan* in this context indicates one who has never experienced sexual intercourse in a valid marriage. See Sa'di Jelbi's *Hashiya* on *Al-'Inaya*, published in the margin of *Fath al-Qadir*, vol. IV, p. 130, and Anderson, op. cit., n. 2.
110. The conditions of *ihsan* are not subject to agreement among the jurists, but we need not go beyond marriage as the most fundamental and important of these. For details, see *Mughni*, p. 161 ff., and 'Uda, vol. II, p. 389 ff.
111. Rida, M. R., *Tafsir al-Manar*, vol. V, p. 25.
112. Shalabi, *Al-Fiqh al-Islami*, p. 201.
113. *Mughni*, pp. 215–216; *Muhalla*, vol. XI, p. 265 ff.
114. 'Uda, op. cit., vol. II, p. 473 ff.
115. *Muhalla*, vol. XI, p. 272 ff.
116. For the other schools' views, see *Mughni*, pp. 216–17; Khirshi's commentary on *Mukhtasar Khalil*, a Maliki text, vol. V, p. 328; *Fath al-Qadir*, vol. IV, p. 190 ff.; Qurtubi, *Tafsir al-Qur'an*, vol. XII, p. 174 ff.
117. For the two views, see 'Uda, vol. I, pp. 266–270.
118. Ibid, pp. 266-270.
119. Qurtubi, *Tafsir*, vol. XII, pp. 201–202; Ibn-Kathir, *Tafsir*, vol. V, p. 67 ff.
120. Ibn Kathir, op. cit.; Qurtubi, *Tafsir*.
121. All *hadd* offences, in fact, result in temporary rejection of the offender's testimony, but here this is ordained as a punishment, while in relation to other *hadd* offences it is a juristic view based on the fact that the *hadd* offences destroy *'adala*, which is the primary condition for the acceptance of testimony.
122. *Muhalla*, vol. XI, pp. 276–281; *Al-Rawd al-Nadir*, vol. IV, p. 493 ff.; *Fath al-Qadir*, vol. IV, p. 190 ff.; *Mukhtasar al-Muzani*, vol. V, p. 168; *Mughni*, vol. VIII, p. 222 ff. It is noteworthy that some of the Hanbali jurists hold the Maliki view, but Ahmad b. Hanbal in his final view preferred the opposite.
123. Khirshi, op. cit., vol. V, p. 329; Mawwaq's commentary on *Mukhtasar Khalil*, vol. VI, p. 301.
124. For example, II: 235.
125. *Al-Rawd al-Nadir*, vol. IV, p. 494; 'Amer, op. cit., p. 161.
126. Kasani, *Badai'*, vol. VII, p. 56 ff.; *Muhalla*, vol. XI, p. 281.
127. For the Hanbali view, see *Mughni*, vol. VIII, pp. 217–218. For the Shafi'i view, see al-Haytami, *Tuhfat al-Muhtaj*, vol. IV, p. 120, with the commentary of Shirawani.
128. Khirshi, op. cit., vol. V, p. 332 ff.; Mawwaq, op. cit., vol. VI, p. 305.
129. *Mishkat al-Masabih*, vol. II, traditions 3567–3570. Bukhari, with the commentary of b. Hajar, vol. XII, p. 72 ff.
130. *Badai'*, vol. VII, p. 52 ff.
131. *Muhalla*, vol. XI, p. 289; see also the references mentioned in fns. 119 and 120.
132. *Muhalla*
133. See the references mentioned above in n. 127.
134. I hold the view which Ibn Hazm expressed in *Al-Muhalla*, vol. XI, pp. 265-300.

135. Sarakhsi, *Mabsut,* vol. XVI, pp. 125–129.
136. Shirbini's commentary on Nawawi's *Minhaj al-Talibin,* vol. IV, p. 403 ff.; Maw-waq, commentary on *Mukhtasar Khalil,* vol. VI, p. 161; *Mughni,* vol. X, pp. 178–181; *Al-Rawd al-Nadir,* vol. IV, pp. 85–87.
137. 'Uda, op. cit., vol. II, pp. 491–492.
138. Mawdudi, *Tafsir Surat al-Nur,* pp. 97–98.
139. See vol. II, pp. 93–111.
140. That is, 'Uda in his two-volume work, *Al-Tashri' al-Jina'i al-Islami,* first published in 1947, in Cairo, and reprinted five times up to 1969; Abu Zahra, *Al Jarima wal-'Uquba,* published about 1959; 'Amer, *Al-Ta'zir,* published in 1955 and reprinted three times up to 1957; A. Ibrahim, *Al-Qisas,* 1944; Abu Haif, *Al-Diya,* 1932.
141. See Howard Jones, *Crime and the Penal System,* pp. 134–145; Jerome Hall, "Science and Reform in Criminal Law," *University of Pennsylvania Law Review,* vol. 100, no. 6, p. 794 ff.; Canham, H. A., *The Nature of Punishment,* p. 19.
142. Jones, op. cit. p. 136.
143. Goodhart, A. L., *English Law and the Moral Law,* p. 93.
144. For example, see the second chapter, entitled "Retribution," in Ted Honderich's *Punishment—The Supposed Justification,* pp. 22–47; Michael Lessnoff, "Two Justifications of Punishment," *The Philosophical Quarterly,* April, 1971; and Jeffrie Murphy, "Three Mistakes about Retributivism," *Analysis,* April 1971.
145. Kant, *Philosophy of Law.*
146. Ibid., pp. 25–34. John Rawls' concept is illustrated in his article "Two Concepts of Rules," *Philosophical Review,* 1955.
147. Rawls, op. cit., p. 7.
148. Michael Lessnoff, op. cit., p. 141; Honderich, op. cit., pp. 22–51.
149. Howard Jones, op. cit. Goodhart, op. cit.
150. See V:33, 38; X:27; XLII:40
151. See, for example, III:145 and LV:60.
152. Ducasse, C. J., "Philosophy and Wisdom in Punishment and Reward," in *Philosophical Perspective on Punishment,* pp. 3–19.
153. Hibbert, *The Roots of Evil,* pp. 19–94; Rolph, C. H., *Common Sense about Crime and Punishment,* p. 102 ff.; Canham, pp. 60, 82–83.
154. The best representatives of this demand are the writers of the Muslim Brotherhood Society in Arab countries and the Islamic Society in Pakistan. The same demand was put forward in the Arab Regional Conference on Crime and the Treatment of Offenders, co-sponsored by the U.N. and the League of Arab States and held in Kuwait on April 4–9, 1970. See the English copy of the final report, pp. 8–14, 18, 23–24, 29. The Conference was held in preparation for the fourth U.N. Conference on the same subject; it was attended by delegates, mostly of the legal profession, representing all the Arab states and Emirates.
155. *Manhaj al-Tarbiya al-Islamiya,* pp. 231–234.
156. vol. 1, p. 636 ff.
157. Baylis, "Immorality, Crime and Treatment," in *Philosophical Perspective on Punishment,* pp. 36–48; cf. Pratt's comments on Ducasse's paper, op. cit., p. 24.
158. Rolph, op. cit., p. 128 ff., where the writer refers to the view of Lord Parker, the former Chief Justice, who told the Cadogan Committee that it is desirable to "retain the (then) existing power to impose sentences of corporal punishment" for certain offences. Also p. 12, fn. (1), where the writer quotes Mr. Harold Sturge, whom he described as "one of the most humane of Magistrates," as saying, "People who say that pain must be taken out of all punishment do not seem to understand much."

159. Ibn al-Qayyim, *Hadi al-Arwah*, p. 273, and *I'lam al Muwaqq'in*, vol. II, p. 100 ff.
160. For a philosophical view concerning the degree of severity, see Michael Clark, "The Moral Gradation of Punishment," *The Philosophical Quarterly*, April 1971, pp. 132–140.
161. Ibn al-Qayyim, op. cit.
162. Bukhari, vol. XII, p. 72 ff.; Muslim, op. cit., vol. V, pp. 114–115.
163. *Fath al-Qadir*, vol. IV, p. 208; Ansari, commentary on *Matn al-Bahja* of Ibn al-Wardi, vol. V, p. 99; *Mughni*, vol. IX, p. 81; *Mudawwanah*, vol. IV, pp. 385, 404.
164. Ansari, op. cit., p. 103.
165. Ansari, op. cit., and 'Uda, vol. I, p. 750, where he quotes *Muhadhdhab*, vol. II, p. 305.
166. Honderich, op. cit., p. 24.
167. For the Shafi'i view, see Ibn Hajar al-Haytami, *Tuhfat al-Muhtaj*, vols. VIII and IX, pp. 401 and 118 respectively; for the Hanbali view see *Mughni*, vol. VII, p. 665.
168. *Mughni*, vol. IX, pp. 46–47.
169. Ibid.; Siyaghi, *Al-Rawd al-Nadir*, vol. IV, pp. 486–487.
170. Honderich, op. cit., p. 26.
171. Quoted from Howard Jones, op. cit., p. 134 ff.
172. *Mishkat al-Masabih*, vol. II, p. 477.
173. Blanshard, B., "Retribution Revised," in *Philosophical Perspective on Punishment*, p. 59.
174. Honderich, op. cit., p. 52, where Jeremy Bentham's *Principles of Penal Law* is quoted.
175. See the working paper prepared by the U.N. Secretariat for the Fourth U.N.C. Conference on Prevention of Crime and Treatment of Offenders, *Organization of Research for Policy Development in Social Defence*, p. 19. The Conference was held in Koyoto, Japan, 17–26 August 1970.
176. Rolph, *Common Sense*, p. 15 ff.
177. Lord Longford, *The Idea of Punishment*, pp. 20–21.
178. Howard Jones, op. cit., pp. 139 ff.
179. Ibid., "Ethics of Penal Action," pp. 26–27.
180. In addition to the above-mentioned references, see Harris' *Criminal Law*, p. 3; Fitzgerald, *Criminal Law and Punishment*, p. 210; Lord Lloyd, *The Idea of Law*, p. 64 ff. A clear summary of the arguments, especially those of a philosophical nature, for and against deterrence may be found in Honderich, op. cit., pp. 52–89.
181. *Al-Ahkam al-Sultaniya*, p. 221.; cf. Levy, *The Social Structure of Islam*, p. 331.
182. See Honderich, op. cit., p. 60.
183. Ibn al-Qayyim, *Hadi al-Arwah*, pp. 268, 272, 279, and his *I'lam al-Muwaqq'in*, vol. II, p. 95 ff.
184. 'Uda, vol. I, p. 712; Shalabi, *Al-Fiqh al-Islami*, pp. 207-208; Abu Zahra, *Al-Jarimah*, p. 14.
185. 'Amer, *Al-Ta'zir*, p. 452. It may be suggested that these figures do not indicate a decrease in the crime rate as much as the authorities' reluctance to report offences to the courts, or the courts' reluctance to pass sentences of amputation. But in a society like that of Saudi Arabia, where nothing like the jury system is known, where every offence is dealt with strictly according to the letter of the law, and where people who carry out their duties do apply, sometimes fanatically, the "Law of God," these figures can be said to indicate a real decrease in the crime rate.
186. The Conference's final report, p. 14.

187.   *The Times,* 8th, April 1971.
188.   Professor Ducasse, C. J., "Philosophy and Wisdom in Punishment" in *Philosophical Perspective in Punishment,* p. 16.
189.   *Fath al-Qadir,* vol. IV, p. 112.
190.   See, for example, Jassas, *Ahkam al-Qur'an,* vol. III, p. 264.
191.   Kasani, *Badai',* vol. VII, p. 60 ff.; 'Uda, vol. I, p. 764 ff.
192.   Abu Dawud, Sunan, vol. IV, pp. 313-314. See also commentary of A.M. Shakir on the *Risalah* of Shafi'i, pp. 171–172.
193.   Shu'rani, *Mizan,* vol. II, pp. 89–91. Coulson, *Succession in the Muslim Family,* p. 176.
194.   Kasani, vol. VII, p. 339; Shirbini, *Mughni al-Muhtaj,* vol. III, p. 24; *Al-Rawd al-Nadir,* vol. V, pp. 119-120.
195.   Al-Keshki, *Al-Mirath al-Muqaran,* p. 51.
196.   Khalil, *Mukhtasar,* with the commentary of Zurqani, vol. VIII, p. 281.
197.   Ibid., and Shu'rani, *Mizan,* vol. II, p. 90. A similar distinction, between "excusable" and "justifiable" homicide, was known in medieval English law. The former, although not a felony, would result in forfeiture of the murderer's property. Justifiable homicide, as in self-defense or execution of public justice, would not lead to forfeiture of the killer's property. See Kenny's *Outlines of Criminal Law,* pp. 127-129.
198.   Kasani, op. cit., p. 339; *Al-Rawd al-Nadir,* pp. 158-159; Shirbini, op. cit., p. 40; Bahuti, op. cit., p. 358; cf.; 'Uda, vol. I, pp. 681-683.
199.   Zurqani, on *Mukhtasar Khalil,* pp. 220-221; Shirbini, op. cit.
200.   See Zurqani, Bahuti and 'Uda, op. cit. For this rule see, Ibn-Nujaym, vol. I, p. 190.
201.   Homicide as a bar to inheritance is excellently surveyed in Coulson, op. cit., pp. 176-185.
202.   Coulson, N.J., *Conflicts and Tensions in Islamic Jurisprudence,* p. 62. See also chapter V of the present work on the law of evidence in criminal cases.
203.   *Al-Rawd al-Nadir,* vol. IV, p. 86; *Mughni,* vol. X, p. 148.
204.   Sarakhsi, *Mabsut,* vol. XVI, p. 132; Shafi'i, *'Umm,* vol. VII, pp. 41–42; Ibn Hazm, *Muhalla,* vol. IV, pp. 431–433.
205.   Howard Jones, op. cit., p. 143 ff.
206.   Ibid., p. 144.
207.   Baylis, C.A., "Immorality, Crime and Treatment," in *Philosophical Perspective on Punishment,* p. 47 ff.; cf. Howard Jones, op. cit., p. 144.
208.   Canham, op. cit., pp. 19.
209.   Howard Jones, op. cit.
210.   For a similar view see 'Uda, op. cit., vol. I, p. 611 ff., and especially 616 ff.
211.   Hadi al-Arwah, op. cit., pp. 268, 272, 273, 279.
212.   Ibid., p. 267.

CHAPTER II

Categorization of the Punishments For Drinking and Apostasy

(Shurb al-Khamr wa al-Ridda)

I. Traditional Islamic Law

The overwhelming majority of Muslim jurists classify the punishments for drinking alcohol and apostasy as *hadd* punishments,[1] and the Western scholars of Islamic law do likewise.[2] The Western scholars in fact follow the views stated in one or the other of the texts on Islamic law. But in order to conduct an objective study of these two penalties, it is neccessary to consult the texts of *ahadith,* especially those compiled by jurists who concentrated their research on *ahadith* of a legal nature (*ahadith al-ahkam*), since both these punishments are prescribed in the Prophet's traditions. The two punishments are not mentioned in the Qur'an, and the Prophet dealt with these crimes in different ways on different occasions.[3] It is threfore a question of understanding and explaning the relevant *ahadith* rather than of writing a treatise on a specific legal clause.

This appears to be a departure from the traditional approach to the various topics of Islamic jurisprudence. The traditional approach is to explain the law as it stands in the medieval legal manuals and to condemn any attempt to reinterpret the authorities and sources of the *Shari'a,* i.e., the Qur'an and the Sunna, on the grounds of the finality and exclusive authority of these manuals as the expression of the *Shari'a.* This, briefly, is the doctrine of *taqlid,* which was established as early as the mid-seventh century A.H.[4] This is a doctrine which has gained very wide support on the basis of the infallibility of the alleged consensus (*ijma'*). Without going any further into this doctrine, we can say that it is becoming increasingly clear that there is an urgent need to reinterpret the principles contained in the Qur'an and the Sunna, if any reform is to take place within the Islamic legal system.[5] Such a view may be criticized as putting forward a description of the law as it ought to be, not as it is. Indeed, such a criticism is sound, but one cannot refrain from pointing out that the Islamic legal manuals are in some cases inadequate. Nevertheless, for those who may not like it, I should say that the views expressed in this chapter are by no means the innovations of an unauthorized student of Islamic law. Fortunately, authoritative jurists have mentioned them, if not explicitly, then at least by implication. But to return to our subject, we will deal first with the punishment for drinking and afterwards with the punishment for apostasy.

II.   The Punishment for Drinking

The drinking of alcoholic beverages or *shurb al-khamr* is one of the topics to which Muslim jurists have given a good deal of attention. Under this heading there are many topics for discussion, e.g., what alcohol is, what it is made of, which kind of alcohol is prohibited *(haram)*, etc. We are unable in this study to discuss all the relevant topics; what we are concerned with here is the punishment for drinking.[6] It is important, however, to note that the Prophet defined *khamr* as "any drink which makes a person drunk," and he declared all drinks of this sort to be forbidden *(haram)*.[7]

In the Qur'an, the drinking of alcohol and various other actions, such as usury *(riba)* and eating the flesh of swine *(akl al-khanzir)*, are simply declared to be forbidden *(haram)*. The drinking of alcohol, however, was the most common of these practices among the Arabs; hence, the Prophet imposed a punishment for it, while the other prohibited acts remained purely civil issues,[8] or as crimes for which there can be a *ta'zir* punishment.[9] As the definition of the *hadd* punishment implies, it can be prescribed only by God. In the one instance in which it was prescribed not by the Qur'an but by the Sunna, the Prophet made it absolutely clear that he was acting according to divine revelation *(wahy)*.[10]

On the other hand, when the Prophet imposed a punishment for drinking, he neither declared that he had imposed it according to revelation nor did he prescribe it in specific terms; that is, he did not fix a definite sentence as the punishment. The Prophetic reports concerned with drinking are related by all the collectors of ahadith, but in none of these reports can one find the Prophet fixing a definite number of lashes as punishment, as is claimed by Muslim jurists.

All the schools of Islamic law consider the drinking of alcohol to be a crime for which a *hadd* punishment is prescribed. Although they disagree about the number of lashes which should be inflicted, they all claim it to have been fixed by the Prophet. According to the Hanafi school, the punishment for drinking is eighty lashes.[11] The same view is held by the Maliki and Hanbali schools.[12] According to another Hanbali view, and to the Shafi'i, Zahiri, and Zaydi schools, the punishment is only forty lashes.[13]

This disagreement about the number of lashes to be inflicted is a result of the differing views ascribed to the Companions of the Prophet. It was reported that the first caliph, Abu Bakr, used to impose forty lashes upon the person who drank; 'Omar did likewise during the first few years of his caliphate. Afterwards, when the number of drinkers increased unprecedently, 'Omar consulted the Prophet's Companions at Madina about the matter. 'Ali or, according to some, 'Abd al-Rahman b. 'Awf suggested that the punishment for drinking should be parallel with the punishment for slander (*qadhf*).[14] In accordance with this report, some jurists hold the view that the *hadd* is forty lashes with another forty lashes as *ta'zir*, while others consider the *hadd* to be eighty lashes, supporting their view by claiming that this number resulted from consensus (*ijma'*).[15]

II. 1. Facts Concerning the Prophetic Traditions Related to the Punishment for Drinking

When we turn to what was reported to have been said or done by the Prophet in relation to this matter, we find that in none of the related reports did the Prophet say that a person who drank should be given forty lashes or eighty lashes. All that is related is that the Prophet ordered the offender to be beaten; "beat him" is the most specific word he is reported to have said.[16] In addition to this, in some, but not in all, cases, the Prophet ordered his companions to reprimand the offender;

again, he took up some dust and threw it in the offender's face although not in every instance. At the same time, when one of his companions reprimanded a drunken man after he had been punished, the Prophet stopped him on the grounds that this might help Satan to induce the offender to commit more sins.[17] In the Prophet's time there were no specific methods of beating offenders. In some instances they were beaten with articles of clothing, hands sandals;[18] while in other cases they were beaten with sticks and palm branches, in addition to sandals.[19]

Moreover, the exact amount of lashes an offender should recieve was not known to the Prophet's Companions. Bayhaqi and Abu Dawud both related that when Abu Bakr, the first caliph, faced the problem of drinking, he asked some of the Prophet's companions about it, but they did not know exactly how many lashes offenders used to receive in the Prophet's time. Accordingly, they guessed at the number and estimated it at about forty lashes. Abu Bakr then imposed this amount as the punishment for drinking.[20] When 'Omar b. al-Khattab was asked by some of the Prophet's companions to review the punishment for drinking as the number of offenders had increased noticeably, he consulted the Prophet's companions at Madina, and it is related that they agreed to raise the number to eighty lashes, making it parallel with the punishment for slander.[21] But that was by no means the only punishment which 'Omar imposed for drinking. There were cases in which he banished the offender, shaved his head, or gave forty or sixty lashes instead of eighty.[22] 'Othman b. 'Affan and 'Ali b. Abi Talib both punished offenders with forty lashes, but it is also related that 'Othman applied a punishment of eighty lashes as well.[23]

Apart from this, it is narrated by reliable transmitters that the Prophet said, "If a person drinks wine, lash him for the first three times and put him to death for the fourth."[24] But when a man was brought before the Prophet for the fourth time, he did not have him put to death but simply ordered him to be beaten.[25]

All these reports show clearly that there was no fixed punishment for drinking in the Prophet's time, nor was such punishment known during the epoch of his Companions. In spite of this, all the schools of Islamic law hold the view that the punishment for drinking is a *hadd* punishment, as was mentioned above. At the same time they claim that the death penalty for a recidivist has been abrogated and is no longer applicable (with the exception of the Zahiri school, which holds the view that a person should be sentenced to death for the fourth offence).[26]

Chapter II **47**

II. 2. The Alleged Consensus

The jurists claim that consensus *(ijma')* places the punishment for drinking in the category of *hadd*. Accordingly, they disapprove of the view expressed by some jurists that the punishment for drinking is a *ta'zir* punishment.[27]

This alleged consensus or *ijma'* concerning various controversial topics is a very common method employed by Muslim jurists for rejecting the views of the opposition.[28] Fortunately, however, it has no legal value.[29] To clarify this point, it is important to understand that consensus or *ijma'*, according to the jurists of *usul al-fiqh* or origins of Islamic law, signifies the agreement of all the eminent jurists of Islam concerning a legal decision at a particular time.[30] In theory, this sort of agreement gives the agreed-upon verdict permanent and infallible legal value.[31] There is much to be said concerning this legal value and about consensus itself. However, here it is sufficient to mention that the authoritative jurists give examples of *ijma'* which in fact show that it was not, as is defined, "the agreement of all" but simply the majority opinion concerning the subject in question.

All the examples represent no more than the views of the majority, and sometimes the majority of one school of law only.[32] This applies even to consensus among the companions of the Prophet; a contemporary scholar, after investigating all the topics concerning which there was a claim of consensus among them, stated that it represented no more than the views of the majority. He concluded that the consensus known to the jurists of Islamic law could not be achieved except by chance or through unanimity concerning a matter such as ritual prayers *(salat)* or fasting during the month of Ramadan.[33]

Therefore, one can say that the claim of consensus regarding the punishment for drinking does not close the door to research into the correct classification of the punishment. Even if there were a consensus (which means the view of the majority), it could not establish a legal verdict which did not exist before, nor could it be of permanent infallible legal value, as the jurists claim.

From the historical facts previously discussed, it is clear that the Prophet's companions held various views concerning the punishment for drinking. Even the Prophet himself imposed different punishments, and in some cases he did not punish the offender at all.[34] Taking these facts into consideration, one can give no credence at all to the views of the schools of Islamic law about the punishment for drinking. All that can be agreed upon is that drinking is an offence, like any other offence, and that it makes a person who commits it liable to a *ta'zir* punishment, which can be defined briefly as an unfixed or discretionary punishment for every offence for which there is no *hadd* punishment or penance.[35] This definition is nearly universally agreed upon, and although all the jurists of all the schools of Islamic law wrote about it, none of them classified the punishment for drinking in the category of *ta'zir*.

The reason for this, as I see it, was the tendency toward unquestioning adoption of the view of one or another of the "imitated scholars" *(taqlid imam)* on the one hand, and the fear of contradicting the common view among jurists on the other; consequently, only those who were not affected by these two considerations stated clearly that the punishment for drinking was actually in the category of *ta'zir*. This view is supported by what b. 'Abbas is related to have said: "The Prophet had not determined a fixed punishment *(hadd)* for the drinking of wine."[36]

II. 3. Individual Juristic Views

Among the jurists who hold this view are Ibn al-Qayyim, Shawkani and Ibn Farhun, and among contemporary scholars Professor Shalabi.[37] Shawkani, Ibn Farhun, and Shalabi were interested in demonstrating that the claim of consensus is incorrect, and they spoke of how different punishments were imposed both by the Prophet himself and by his companions.[38] Ibn al-Qayyim explained that this diversity of punishments means that the punishment is in the category of *ta'zir*, and he considered the verdict in the *hadith* which ordered the offender to be sentenced to death as the most severe kind of *ta'zir* which can be inflicted among other punishments suitable for the recidivist offender.[39]

This *hadith*, in my opinion, shows that in the case of the recidivist offender the court may go beyond the limits laid down for *ta'zir* punishments, as narrated in another *hadith* transmitted by Bukhari, Muslim, Tirmidhi, Ibn Majah, and Abu Dawud.[40] There are different views about what this *hadith* implies, but whatever one thinks about it, it does limit the punishments of *ta'zir* for the less important sins to ten lashes. As for the more serious sins, the Prophet made it possible to exceed this limit when necessary for the public interest *(maslaha)*.

By understanding the matter in this way, one need not hold a view which contradicts the Prophet's practice, that is, the view which claims that the punishment for drinking is a *hadd* punishment, nor the view that the Prophet abrogated the verdict in which he prescribed the death penalty for the fourth crime. This view is unsubstantiated, and is based simply on the fact that no one has ever been sentenced to death for drinking after the third time.[41] At the same time, our view concerning this punishment avoids the danger inherent in the extreme view of the Zahiris, who consider the death penalty for the fourth crime of drinking as a *hadd* punishment. [42]

To summarise what has been said in this section, one can say that in Islamic law the drinking of alcohol is a serious sin. no punishment is mentioned in the Qur'an for this sin; it is declared to be forbidden (*haram*) but nothing more. As wine-drinking was a common habit among the Arab tribesmen, the Prophet imposed different kinds of punishment, primarily the beating of drinkers.[44] Most of lthe jurists claim that there is a *hadd* punishment for this sin, but this claim has been shown to be invalid.

One remaining argument for the majority view is that the word *hadd* refers to the offence rather than to the punishment; hence, as drinking is declared in the Qur'an to be *haram,* it is right to consider it as a *hadd* offence. But this argument ignores the fact that an offence in the category of *hadd* is, by definition, an offence for which a fixed punishment has been prescribed in the Qur'an or the Prophet's Sunna; if it were otherwise, all prohibited acts and omissions would be, or are, offences of *hudud.* Such an opinion has never been, and can never be, defended. It is worth mentioning that recently the punishment for drinking was referred to as a "penalty stated in the Qur'an,"[45] but this is obviously an error. Accordingly, nothing can prevent the law-maker in a Muslim society from prescribing any suitable punishment for this sin, on the same grounds on which he can establish a punishment for any sin which has become, in given circumstances, common enough among the people to threaten the existence of the society, the good of the majority, or the public interest.

III. The Punishment for Apostasy

The Arabic word for apostasy is *"ridda"* or *"irtidad,"* which literally means "turning back." The former is usually used to signify turning back from Islam to another religion or to unbelief, while the latter has this meaning in addition to others; a person who forsakes Islam for unbelief or for another religion is called a *murtadd* (apostate).[46]

The common view among Muslim jurists, as well as among Western orientalists, is that apostasy from Islam is a crime for which the death penalty is prescribed. The majority of the Muslim jurists, it has been remarked, classify this punishment as being in the *hadd* category.[47]

It has already been noted that *hadd* punishments are punishments determined by the Qur'an or the Sunna of the Prophet, and that they are to be carried out if guilt is proven. Now in order to determine whether or not apostasy is a crime for which Islamic law has prescribed the alleged *hadd* punishment, one should consult the verses of the Qur'an, and the ahadith dealing with the subject, as well as the practice of the Prophet's Companions, which indicates how they understood both the Qur'an and the Sunna in relation to the matter. In this way it can be seen whether what is commonly accepted among Muslim jurists is correct or not.

III. 1. Apostasy in the Qur'an

Apostasy is mentioned in the Qur'an in thirteen verses contained in different surahs, but in none of these verses can one find any mention of punishment to be carried out in this world. On the contrary, all that these verses contain is the assurance that the apostate will be punished in the Hereafter.[48] Some examples of such verses may be useful to demonstrate this fact. Surah XVI, verse 106 states, "Whoever rejects faith in God after believing in Him, excepting under compulsion while his heart remains firm in faith—but such as open their breast to unbelief, on them is wrath from God and theirs will be a dreadful penalty."[49] This verse was revealed during the late Meccan period, and it is clear from the words that the apostate is threatened only with punishment in the next life.

In Madina, where the Prophet established his state shortly after his migration *(hijra),* Surah II was revealed. In this Surah the mention of apostasy was also accompanied by the warning that the apostate would be punished in the next world (verse 217). At Madina the Prophet also received the revelation of the third surah of the Qur'an, in which aspostasy was again mentioned in many verses, but always with the declaration that the apostates would be punished, not in this world but in the next (verses 86–91). In yet another Madinian revelation, the Qur'an declared: "O you who believe! if one of you should turn back from his religion, then God will bring a people whom He shall love, and they too shall love Him'' (V: 54). In this verse the *murtadd* is certainly exempt from any sort of punishment in this life.

At the same time, one can say that the death penalty for apostasy— especially when it is considered as a *hadd* punishment—contradicts the Qur'anic principle law states in Surah II, verse 256, which proclaims ''No compulsion in religion.'' Ibn Hazm, to avoid this criticism, claimed that this verse had been abrogated and that compulsion is allowed in religion; consequently, according to him, the punishment for apostasy does not contradict the Qur'an.[50] However, this claim is invalid, since Qur'anic scholars have established the abrogated verses and this verse is not among them.[51] Accordingly, one can say with the *Encyclopaedia of Islam* that ''In the Qur'an the apostate is threatened with punishment in the next world only.''[52]

III. 2. The Sunna and Apostasy

It is a common practice among Muslim jurists, when introducing their discussion of apostasy, to quote one or the other of the Qur'anic verses dealing with the subject. At the same time, the strongest evidence they use to prove that apostasy is a *hadd*-type offence punishable by the death penalty is that of two prophetic reports which we shall now examine along with the report about the group from the tribe of 'Ukal to which reference was made in the first chapter of this study.[53]

As for the report concerning the 'Ukal group, some of the Muslim jurists claim that they were punished because of their apostasy.[54] The same view is held by some Western orientalists. Zwemre, in his book *The Law of Apostasy in Islam,* describes the case of the 'Ukal as the earliest case of apostasy. He quotes Muslim concerning it, and comments that the text shows how "the earliest apostates were tortured by Muhammad."[55]

On the other hand, the prevalent view among Muslim jurists is that the case of this group of 'Ukal and 'Urayna was a case of *hiraba* (armed robbery) and it was for this crime that they were punished.[56] The text itself demonstrates this very clearly. It is true that most jurists classify them as apostates *(murtaddun)* and rebels against God and His Prophet *(muharibun),* but the term apostate came to be used incidentally or because the people of 'Ukal and 'Urayna, in addition to their having committed the crime of *hiraba,* also rejected Islam. In any case, it is universally agreed that this incident has noting to do with the punishment ordained in Islamic law for apostasy. Accordingly, nothing can be inferred from this report to help in determining the punishment for apostasy.

Another Prophetic report commonly used in discussing the subject is the *hadith* transmitted by Bukhari, Muslim, and Abu Dawud: "The life of a Muslim may be taken only in three cases, i.e., in the case of a married adulterer, one who has killed a human being *(qatal nafsan)*, crucified, Islam, forsakes his religion and separates himself from his community *(al-murtaddu 'an dinihi al-mufariqu lil-jama'a)*.[57] On the basis of this hadith the jurists maintain that the Prophet allowed the death penalty for a Muslim if he apostatized.[58] But this report was narrated by Abu Dawud in different words, in which the Prophet explained what he meant by "one who forsakes his religion and separates himself from his community." In the latter version, such an individual is described as "a man who went out (from the community) to fight against God and His Prophet, and should then be put to death, crucified or imprisoned."[59] In order to reconcile the words of this *hadith* with the words of the Qur'an (Surah V, verses 33-34), Ibn Taymiyya explained that the crime referred to in this hadith is the crime of *hiraba* (armed robbery). He holds that this is an explanation of the words in the former version, "one who forsakes his religion . . ."

Accordingly, this *hadith* has nothing to do with the case of simple apostasy, i.e., apoastasy which is not accompanied by fighting against God and His Prophet.[60] In other words, this report indicates that anyone who commits the crime of *hiraba* in fact separates himself from his religion because a Muslim would never commit such a crime. Again, the law for apostasy cannot be inferred from this *hadith*.

The strongest emphasis is laid on a *hadith* narrated by Ibn 'Abbas in which the Prophet said, "Whoever changes his religion, kill him;"[61] it is primarily on the strength of this *hadith* that jurists based their view that an apostate should be sentenced to death. Their work on the subject generally[62] shows them to interpret the words, "Kill him," as a grammatical imperative *sighat alamr*, that is, as an order which must be carried out.

In his book, *The Religion of Islam*, Muhammad 'Ali defended the view that Islam knows of no death penalty for apostasy unless the apostate joins forces with the enemies of Islam in a state of actual war, in which case he is killed not because of his apostasy but simply like any other fighter against Islam *(muharib)*[63] He supported his view by explaining that unless we apply this limitation to its meaning, the preceding *hadith* canno be reconciled with other *hadith* or with the principles laid down in the Qur'an.[64] Moreover, the wording of this *hadith* is very broad, including any change from one religion to another, implying that even a non-Muslim who becomes a Muslim, or a Jew who becomes a Christian must be killed. On these grounds Muhammad 'Ali stated that the hadith cannot be accepted without placing a limitation upon its meaning.[65]

This last statement is already agreed upon by the majority. All schools, with the exception of the Zahiri and some Shafi'i jurists, allow that a non-Muslim who changes from his original religion to any other is not to be harmed, while a Muslim who leaves Islam for any other religion should be sentenced to death unless he returns to Islam.[66] The Hanafi school puts another limitation on the meaning of this *hadith* by applying it to male apostates only. According to their view, a female apostate is not liable to the death penalty since she is not in any position to fight against Islam, which is the ostensible the reason for putting to death an apostate.[67]

But these limitations on the meaning of the above hadith still do not lead to the conclusion of Muhammad 'Ali, i.e., that an apostate cannot be put to death unless he is in a real state of war against Islam. A careful and objective study of the subject, avoiding the apologists' view which influenced Muhammad 'Ali, may lead to an entirely different conclusion.

IV. A View Concerning Apostasy

It has already been mentioned that nothing in the Qur'anic verses cited can be taken as a justification for the death penalty as a *hadd* punishment for apostasy. As for the Sunna, it has been said that one of the two reports concerned has nothing to do with the point in question. However, the other *hadith*, in which the death penalty was ordered for the apostate, was understood as a clear command prescribing the death penalty as a *hadd* punishment for apostasy.

The jurists have usually tried to avoid the execution of the punishments as far as possible, either on the principle of doubt (*shubuhat*) or through the law of proof. Yet in relation to apostasy they have extended the cases in which the punishment can be carried out, through broadening the words and acts which might be considered as formal apostasy, to an extent entirely beyond the actual meaning of apostasy, the changing one's religion.[68]

The jurists were led to this, I feel, by the emphasis placed on the question of faith by Islamic law and the feeling that, after changing his religion, an individual might become an example which could be imitated. Moreover, it is common knowledge among Muslims that nothing is worse than becoming a disbeliever after being a Muslim. The jurists were also influenced by the literal meaning of the report which ordered the apostate to be put to death. I will focus my inquiry into the punishment for apostasy on this last consideration.

To understand an Islamic legal clause, one should consult the authorities on the origins of Islamic law (*'ulama' al-usul*). The point to be sure of here is the meaning of the imperative mood (*sighat al-amr*) in Arabic generally and in Qur'anic and Prophetic usage in particular.

The jurists who have written concerning the subject have indicated that the imperative may be used in sixteen different ways; among them are recommendation, inimitability, threat, permission, and the literal meaning of the imperative, which signifies a command or an order.[69] And because in the *hadith* concerned the imperative mood is indeed considered to be a command or order, jurists have generally placed the punishment for apostasy in the *hadd* category. The imperative mood, however, cannot be said to be resttricted to a single meaning unless there is factual evidence to support it.

The factual evidence in the case in question by no means supports the view that this imperative usage indicates an order. In the first place, the Qur'anic verses concerned did not prescribe any punishment for apostasy but simply declared it to be a great sin. Secondly, the Prophet who said these words about apostates never himself had an apostate put to death. There were some cases in which people apostasized after converting to Islam, but the Prophet never ordered any of them to be killed.[70] On the contrary, Bukhari and Muslim[71] related that "an Arab (a bedouin) came to the Prophet and accepted Islam; then fever overtook him while he was still at Madina, so he came to the Prophet and said, 'Give back my pledge,' but the Prophet refused; then he came the next day and said to the Prophet, 'Give me back my pledge,' and the Prophet refused. The Arab did the same a third day and the Prophet refused.'' The report goes on to say that the man afterwards left Madina unharmed. This is a clear case of apostasy in which there was no punishment. It is clear from the words of the report that the bedouin was seeking to return to his old religion, or at least to leave Islam, but in spite of this he went away unharmed.[72]

Another case of apostasy is reported in which the apostates were a group of Jews who had accepted Islam and then returned to their original religion; the case is mentioned in the Qur'an III: 71-73. These Jews would pretend that they had accepted Islam in the first part of the day and show that they did not believe in it at the end of the day. This was done, according to the Qur'an, in order to undermine the confidence of newly- converted Muslims. At that time the Prphet was the ruler of Medina. Consequently, one cannot imagine how such people could have done this under a government which punishes apostary with the death penalty, while they were not in fact, punished in any way.

This is the factual evidence relating to the *hadith* concerned, and accordingly, I understand apostasy to be punishable by *ta'zir* punishment and not by *hadd*. The words, "kill him," in the *hadith* concerned, however, make it possible for the judge to go beyond the limits of *ta'zir* laid down in another previously-mentioned *hadith*,[74] the one in which the Prophet ordered a man found drinking for the fourth time to be sentenced to death as a *ta'zir* punishment.[75]

In spite of the view that apostasy is punishable by a *hadd* punishment, that is, by the death penalty, there are jurists who consider its punishment to be *ta'zir*. This view was expressed during different eras of Islamic law. During the caliphate of 'Omar, a man came to him from a section of the army which was fighting for Islam, and the Caliph asked him what had been done with some people who were known to have apostatized. The man replied that they had been killed, the requirement of the *hadd* punishment. 'Omar then said that if he could have taken them in peace it would have been the best thing for him. The man asked 'Omar what he would have done if he had taken them in peace, and the Caliph replied that he would have asked them to return to Islam and if they refused he would have imprisoned them.[76] Imprisonment is clearly not one of the *hadd* punishments, and it could not have been inflicted on these apostates except as *ta'zir*.

Among the followers of the Prophet's companions, Ibrahim al-Nakh'i (d. 95 A.H.) and Sufyan al-Thawri (d. 161 A.H.) held the view that the apostate should be invited back to Islam and should never be sentenced to death.[77] Baji, the distinguished Maliki jurist, made it very clear that apostasy is "a sin for which there is no *hadd* punishment."[78] A sin of this sort can be punished only by a *ta'zir* punishment. Finally, Ibn Taymiyya stated categorically that the punishment for apostasy is a *ta'zir* punishment; it is or should be a severe punishment, but still it is in the category of *ta'zir*.[79]

Moreover, the jurists who hold that the apostate should be sentenced to death do not all agree that this is a *hadd* punishment; they sometimes call it *hadd* and sometimes not.[80] According to the Hanafi, Shafi'i, and Zahiri school, the death penalty for apostasy is a *hadd* punishment,[81] and, although according to the Hanbali school it is not a *hadd* punishment, still an apostate should be killed because of his unbelief *(kufr)*. However, Ibn Qudamah, in *Al-Mughni*, did not categorize the punishment as *ta'zir* or as anything else.[82]

The Islamic penal system recognizes three kinds of punishments: *hadd* (fixed punishment), *qisas* (retaliation), and *ta'zir* (discretionary punishments). The second is certainly out of the question here, and since it cannot be proved that the punishment for apostasy pertains to the category of *hadd,* it can only be understood as a *ta'zir* punishment. The preceding remarks about the reasons for claiming drinking to be punishable by *hadd* also apply here and need not be repeated.

To sum up, the Qur'an prescribes no punishment in this life for apostasy. The Prophet never sentenced a man to death for it. Some of the companions of the Prophet recognized apostasy as a sin for which there was a *ta'zir* punishment, as did some jurists. Actually, Islamic law considers apostasy as the most major sin and the limits for *ta'zir* are not, in its case, of binding force. Thus, a court may either sentence an apostate to death, imprison him, or prescribe whatever other punishment it thinks appropriate. Also, the law-makers of a Muslim community may enact whatever punishment they feel to be suitable for this offence.

V. A Survey of the Punishments for Drinking and Apostasy

The conclusion reached in the two preceding sections was that drinking and apostasy cannot be categorized as crimes for which there are *hadd* punishments. While both are sins which a Muslim is urged strongly to avoid, a *ta'zir* punishment is prescribed for both under Islamic law, and such a punishment, by its nature, is expected to vary according to the culprit's personal character, the circumstances, the time, and the manner in which the crime was committed.

Some may question the basis for prescribing punishments for these two sins. In fact Islamic criminal law knows of no distinction between sin and crime, although such a distinction is well-established among Western thinkers and in the Western literature in both law and philosophy. But as the function of *ta'zir* in Islamic law is to provide a legal sanction for every sin for which there is neither a *hadd* punishment nor penance *(kaffara)*,[84] the distinction between sin and crime, or between criminal action and moral guilt, no longer exists.

Accordingly, the use of the word sin *(ma'siya)* in this text and in Islamic legal writing as well, should be understood to refer to an action or omission for which there is no *hadd* punishment or penance, but which makes its doer liable to a *ta'zir* punishment.

This question, therefore, should be rephrased. Why, it could be asked, did the Prphet order penalties for some sins, while other were left to the discretion of judges or rulers? A simple explanation might be that he ordered punishment for the major sins in order to draw the Muslims' attention to them, and so that those who committed them would not go unpunished. While the Qur'an proclaims that there will be a grave punishment for sins in the Hereafter, this might lead people, as it has led some, to say that nothing should be done about these sins in this world or through the state's authority. To prevent this, the Prophet called attention to some major misdeeds and taught his followers that such conduct must be punished. Major misdeeds can be understood to mean two principal things: (1) an act or omission which may become so widespread among people as to threaten the public interest, and (2) an act or omission which is likely to harm a human being either physically or mentally, the spread of which is undesirable. In other words, any sort of conduct which threatens the existence or the well-being of the community, either directly or indirectly, may be considered a major sin in this sense.

The purpose behind punishing such conduct is merely to deter people from indulging in it; as was shown earlier, deterrence is one of the major purposes of punishment in Islamic law.[85] But in this context deterrence plays the role of a mere means, while in its earlier context it could be regarded as an end in itself. The kinds of conduct mentioned previously should not exist in a Muslim society; at the same time it is the right and responsibility of the government to safeguard the society from such conduct or such harm where these exist, and the imposition of penalties or punishments is one of the means by which society can be so safeguarded.

The protection of society is universally accepted as a purpose of punishment.[86] It assumes that crime is wrong done against the public interest,a threat of the preservation of order which should be prevented. On the other hand, it is for the good of the individual not to repeat this sort of action, even if the means of preventing him are necessarily painful.[87]

The protection of society is, I think, the purpose behind such punishments as those in question, i.e., the punishments for drinking and apostasy, for Islamic law has prescribed deterrent punishments for such crimes or misdeeds in order to safeguard Muslim society from their consequences.[88] To support this view, one has only to demonstrate what effect these misdeeds can have upon the community and how they can harm its existence or well-being. For the sake of clarity, this topic is divided into two subsections.

V. 1. Drinking

Alcohol is as old, no doubt, as civilized man; nearly every society appears to have discovered it in one or another of its many forms.[89] In Western social life, alcohol has an honored and traditional place, so much so that Professor Kessel and Dr. Walton state at the beginning of their book, *Alcoholism*, that "it is the abstainer who strikes us as the more abnormal."[90]

As for the reasons behind this universal habit of drinking, the same authority declared: "With alcohol we offer hospitality and display our sociability . . . over a glass we enjoy old friends and make new ones, proclaim our loyalties, discuss affairs, negotiate and seal bargains . . . strangers relax and mingle if alcohol is provided . . . drinks will make them (the strangers) socialize . . . they will become less inclined to judge others critically. Oiling the social wheels is at the centre of society's approbation of regulated drinking."[91]

The situation was very much the same among the Arabs. The Qur'an indicates that *khamr* (wine or alcohol) has some usefulness,[92] but the same verse goes on to state that the drinking of it is a great sin and that its harm outweighs its utility. In a later revelation this great sin was explained in terms of the effect which Satan has on those who drink, and alcohol was accordingly declared to be forbidden (*haram*).

The Qur'an terms alcohol an impure thing or *rijs*. It may be questioned whether this is the actual reason for its prohibition, but the Qur'anic verse in which alcohol is so classified gives the reasons for this classification. It states: "Satan only seeks to cast enmity and hatred among you by means of drinking and gambling, and to turn you from remembrance of God and worship" (V:91).

Hence, one can say that the evil effect of alcohol on human beings led to its classification as an impure thing and to its prohibition. This view is borne out by the fact that the above verse was revealed and alcoholic drinks were declared to be forbidden when a group of Muslims, after getting drunk, engaged in a fight among themselves.[94] It is therefore correct to state that drinking was prohibited in order to protect the society and its individuals from its harmful effects.[95]

However, the prohibition and the explanation for it were accepted among Muslims, and they still accept it, simply as the will of God, Who has the right to determine for His creatures what is right and what is wrong, or, in the Islamic expression, what is lawful (*halal*) and what is unlawful (*haram*).[96] Accordingly, Muslim writers have said very little about either the utility or the harmful effect of alcohol-drinking.[97] In fact, the vast majority of Muslims, if not all, disapprove of it simply because it is not allowed by Islam.

In recent times, scientific research has made a valuable contribution to our knowledge about the harmful effects of alcohol. Doctors, criminologists, psychotherapists, and sociologists have all demonstrated that alcohol has a considerable effect on both physical and mental health, and consequently on criminality and the crime rate as well. An important chapter of Kessel and Walton's book, *Alcoholism,* deals with the harmful effects of alcohol on the brain and the body. These effects range from malnutrition to the destruction of brain cells. The symptoms of each disorder are different, with differing chances of recovery; while some may recover completely, others may suffer permanent damage.[98]

Dr. Frances Smart has discussed some cases which prove a clear causal relationship between alcoholic addiction and the committing of crime. In one of these cases, a man of forty-two had episodes of compulsive arson; those episodes always followed fairly heavy drinking; the man "only thought about fire-raising when he was in a particular mood, and this only came on after he had been drinking."[99] Dr. Smart refers to other cases which connect drinking with the committing of crimes but this case is the most serious.[100]

The relationship between drunkenness and crimes, is also discussed in different parts of Hermann Mannheim's distinguished work, *Comparative Criminology.*[101] In this book the relationship between drinking and motor accidents is discussed, and reference is made to a report by the British Medical Research Council concerning the effects of small doses of alcohol on driving, which indicate that drivers under the influence of alcohol are responsible for about 500 deaths and for 2000 to 3000 injuries annually in The United Kingdom.[102]

The connection of alcohol with cases of homicide and juvenile delinquency is also discussed. Concerning the latter, the same authority quotes some researchers' results which prove an indisputable relationship between alcoholic parents and children who commit crimes.[103] In relation to homicide, drinking was the cause or motive of 90 out of a total of 551 murders committed in England and Wales during the twenty years ending in 1905.[104] Mannheim also refers to some researchers who confirmed the relationship between alcohol and homicide.[105] Statistics cited by C. Hibbert also prove a very close relationship between drinking and crime in various Western countries, including the United States.[106]

What has been said concerning the harmful effects of drinking on both the individual and the community, and especially about its relationship with crime, is enough to support the prohibitionists' view. These facts were completely unknown at the time when Islam prohibited drinking, but they have often been cited in recent writings to justify the *hadd* punishment that was alleged to have been applied for it.[107] A better approach, in my opinion, would be that, in view of the clear evidence of the harm which may befall the individual who drinks and his society,[108] the intervention of the state by means of punishment for drinkers is justifiable. However, the form this punishment should take is to be determined in each individual society in a way which corresponds to its actual needs and particular circumstances.

As far as classical Islamic law is concerned, these facts have nothing to do with the punishment dealt with in the legal manuals, for that punishment was established on religious ground, i.e., in accordance with the teachings of the Prophet, or rather of his companions *(sahaba)*. But as far as modern Muslim societies are concerned, such facts were the grounds on which the prohibition of alcohol and its production and trade were introduced, in Kuwait, for example.[109] However, it is interesting that the punishment prescribed by the penal code of Kuwait is not the alleged *hadd* punishment, in spite of the strong influence of conservative individuals and groups in that country; the punishment fixed by the penal code varies according to the crime committed. Its minimum is six months imprisonment or 50 dinars fine, and the maximum penalty is ten years imprisonment or 300 dinars fine. Such penalties can be classified as *ta'zir* but not as *hadd* punishments, and they have proved to be successful in serving the aim of protecting society from the dangerous effects of drinking.[110]

To summarize, we can say that the principle which underlies the penalty for drinking in Islamic law is the protection of society; for clearly society must protect itself against the spread of such a habit because of its unquestionably harmful effects and also because of its established relationship to crime. Reference has been made to the successful experiment of introducing a punishment for drinking and trafficking in alcohol in Kuwait, whereby the so-called *hadd* punishment for drinking in a largely conservative Muslim society was replaced by a *ta'zir* punishment in terms of fines and imprisonment.

Attention may be given here to the similarity between the offence of drinking and that of drug addiction. It is common knowledge that drug addiction is a habit which, through its harmful effects on individuals, endangers society. In the West, and throughout most of the world, the campaign against drug addiction is now stronger and more far-reaching than ever. Yet the habit is continues to increase at an alarming rate.

Muslim jurists who have dealt with the problem of drug addiction agree concerning the prohibition of drugs, but they disagree as to the penalty for their misuse.[111] While the Islamic legal manuals deal primarily with the addiction to *cannabis* or hashish, the agreed-upon prohibition evidently covers all other drugs. To return to the case of Kuwait, it is interesting to note that under the Kuwaiti penal code drugs are treated in the same section as alcohol and the related offences are punished by very similar penalties.[112]

V. 2. Apostasy

Apostasy has been discussed less than drinking. The subject is completely unknown to Western writers; some orientalists have written about it, but only to explain the Muslim point of view, as they have understood it. It was dealt with in the *Jewish Encyclopaedia*, but merely as a matter of historical importance and without any attempt to explain the punishment's rationale in Jewish law.

It has already been mentioned that Muslim writers hold two different views concerning it. The more common is that the punishment for apostasy is the death penalty and that it falls in the category of *hadd*. A less common, but well-documented, view is that is a *ta'zir* punishment which may be as severe as the death penalty and which must, like all *ta'zir* punishments, be determined according to the particular circumstances of each case.

However, none of the supporters of either of these two views has tried to question the purpose behind prescribing a punishment for such conduct. The holders of the first view did not analyse its purpose because it was, according to them, a *hadd* punishment which need not be widely discussed but was simply to be accepted as the will of God. Those who hold the second view do so unquestioningly, because they concentrate on presenting evidence and proof of their point of view. Although in some of the Islamic law texts, especially of the Hanafi school, one can find some general comments about the reasons underlying the punishment for apostasy, such general observations do not contribute much toward achieving the aim of an attempted modern legal study.

It was assumed at the beginning of this section that the principle underlying the punishment for drinking and apostasy was the protection of society against the potential or actual harm of such acts. This has been adequately proved with regard to drinking. Whether or not it is also correct with regard to apostasy is the subject of the next pages.

Some preliminary observations are necessary here. The first concerns the widely held principle among Muslims that Islam provides a total system of life, starting from birth, extending throughout every moment of life. Matters such as infant-feeding and child-rearing, marriage and divorce, legacy and inheritance, bargains and contracts, war and peace, international relations, the treatment of minorities, and many other aspects are governed in one way or another by legal rules in the sources of Islamic law. Secondly, Muslims, and especially Muslim jurists, consider all these aspects as having the same importance as, let us say, ritual prayer (*salat*) and fasting. Hence, any problem which arise should be treated and solved in the way recommended by, or at least in harmony with, the related rules in Islamic law.[113] Accordingly, all aspects of Islamic law should be taken and accepted as a unit, one total and indivisible system.[114] With regard to these principles, some jurists hold that if the ruler (or the government) acts against some of the rules of Islamic law, he should be advised by the learned men to rectify the error by complying with them and to remedy the harm, if any, brought about by his actions. If he, or the government, does so the matter is over. But i not, the believers should fight for their right to be governed in accordance with the divinely ordained rules of Islam.[115]

A Muslim state should be shaped in this way and the various authorities in it should be given their power in accordance with, and not ouside, the limits of the law of Islam. This principle is recognized as a fundamental one, to the extent that all conflicts and challenges which have been raised against the rules of one or another Muslim country have been connected with it.[116] Recently, the demand to adopt this principle was behind the conflict between the Islamic movement and some of the Arab governments.[117]

It is quite natural, according to such principles, to consider loyalty to the laws of the community as a highly necessary condition for the enjoyment of the protection of the law and the authority of the state. At the same time, it is natural to consider disloyalty as a reason for justifying the deprivation of such protection. This was the explanation given for the punishment for apostasy by some modern writers on the subject.[118]

The question which remains is how disloyalty to the Islamic law could be an act harmful to society and how punishment for it can be justified. For this point we can give two explanations. The first one relates to the case referred to in the Qur'an,[119] i.e., the case of the Jews who would pretend that they had accepted Islam at the beginning of the day, while at the end of it, they would say that they had rejected it in order to weaken the commitment of newly-converted Muslims. The second is the case of those who apostatize from Islam and join hands with its enemies in an actual state of war, or who unite people against Islam or the Muslim state and then fight against it.

Both cases are clearly harmful to the society. While the former encourages the people to reject the law and order of the society (which is based on its religion) by rejecting the religion itself, the latter involves the waging of war, or helping those who wage it, against the apostate's own state. In both cases punishment is, I believe justified, in order to protect society from the harm brought by the apostate's action. However in any other case, that is, in cases of simply change of one's religion, punishment cannot be justified. One can understand, therefore, the Hanafi school's view of punishing the male apostate only, leaving the female apostate unpunished, because she is not able to fight against the Muslim state, which the male apostate is able to do .[121] This view was understood by some as being based on the "potentiality to fight;" consequently, it was not accepted.[122] But the fact is that it is based on what usually happens and not on the mere potentiality. The proof is that some of the Hanafi jurists stated that "an apostate could not be punished for mere unbelief, but to prevent the mischief of war" which follows his rejection of Islam.[123]

Finally, the concept of punishing a person who displays disloyalty toward his country is well-known in all legal systems. In modern legal systems, this may be called treason or conspiracy, but the concept is almost always the same.[124]

To summarize, Islam is regarded by Muslims not as a mere religion but as a complete system of life. Its rules are prescribed not only to govern the individual's conduct but also to shape the basic laws and public order in the Muslim state. Accordingly, apostasy from Islam is classified as a crime for which *ta'zir* punishment may be applied. The punishment is inflicted in cases in which the apostate is a cause of harm to the society, while in those cases in which an individual simply changes his religion the punishment is not to be applied.[125] But it must be remembered that unthreatening apostasy is an exceptional case, and the common thing is that apostasy is accompanied by some harmful actions against the society or state. A comparison between the concept of punishing those who commit treason in modern systems of law and those who commit apostasy in Islamic law would be useful. Assuredly, the protection of society is the underlying principle in the punishment for apostasy in the legal system of Islam.

NOTES

1. See, for example, Kasani, *Badai' al-Sanai'*, vol. VII, p. 33 ff.; Shirwani and 'Abbadi, *Hawashi Tuhfat al-Muhtaj*, vol. IX, p. 166 ff.; 'Uda, op.cit., vol. I, p 648 ff., and vol. II, p. 496 ff.
2. See Coulson, *History*, p. 124. For drinking, see J. Schacht, *An Introduction to Islamic Law*, pp. 175, 179. For apostasy see S. M. Zwemre, *The Law of Apostasy in Islam*.
3. This is particularly applicable to the crime of drinking.
4. Shalabi, *Usul al-Fiqh*, pp. 22–31, and his *Al-Madkhal lil Fiqh al-Islami*, p. 138 ff
5. A clear though brief account of this view is to be found in Coulson, op.cit., pp 202–203. For the invalidity of the alleged consensus, see Shalabi, *Usul al-Fiqh*, op cit.
6. For details, see vol. I, *Encyclopedia of Islamic Jurisprudence*, Ministry of Awqaf Kuwait, 1969.

7. Muslim, with the commentary of al-Nawawi, published in the margin of *Al-Bukhari*, vol. X, p. 172.
8. Coulson, op.cit., pp. 11–12.
9. The definition of *ta'zir* punishment was extended to deal with every crime for which there is no *hadd* punishment or penance *(kaffara)*.
10. See what was said previously about death by stoning as a punishment for a married adulterer.
11. Kasani, *Badai'*, vol. VII, pp. 57, 60. Ibn al-Humam, *Fath al-Qadir*, vol. VI, p. 183 ff.
12. For the Maliki view, see *Sharh al-Hattab* on *Mukhtasar Khalil*, vol. VI, p. 317, and *Sharh al-Mawwaq* in the margin of the same book, p. 317. For the Hanbali view, see al-Ruhaybani, *Matalib Uli al-Nuha*, vol. VI, p. 212.
13. *Mughni*, vol. VIII, p. 307. For the Shafi'i view, see Nawawi, *Minhaj al-Talibin*, vol. IV, p. 174; for the Zahiri view, *Al-Muhalla*, vol. XI, p. 365; for the Zaydi school, *Rawd*, vol. IV, p. 505 ff.
14. Bayhaqi, *Al-Sunan al-Kubra*, vol. VIII, p. 320.
15. Shawkani, *Nayl al-Awtar*, vol. VII pp. 138–143.
16. A collection of the reports concerned will be found in Shawkani, op.cit., p. 138, and *Mishkat al-Masabih*, vol. II, pp. 304–308.
17. See *Mishkat al-Masabih*, especially pp. 305 and 308.
18. Ibid., and what is related by Ahmad b. Hanbal, Bukhari, and Abu Dawud.
19. See ibid., and Shawkan i, op.cit. p. 138, where Ahmad b. Hanbal and Bukhari are quoted.
20. Bayhaqi, op.cit. pp. 319–320, and Abu-Dawud, *Al-Sunan*, with the treatise of 'Awnu al-Ma'bud, vol. 4, p. 284.
21. *Al-Sunan*, p.320, and *Nayl al-Awtar*, pp. 140-142.
22. *Muhalla*, vol. XI, p. 365.
23. *Muhalla*, and *Nayl al-Awtar*, pp. 138–139.
24. Abu Dawud, op.cit., pp. 280–282, and *Nayl al-Awtar*, p. 146–147, where Ahmad b. Hanbal, Bukhari, Muslim and Tirmidhi are quoted.
25. *Abu Downd* and *Mishkat al-Masabih*, p. 305
26. See the above-mentioned references in notes 11, 12 and 13 and *Muhalla*, pp. 365-370.
27. Shawkani, *op.cit.*, p. 142.
28. Shalabi, *Ta'lil al-Ahkam*, pp. 5–6.
29. Ibid, pp. 5-6
30. Khallaf, *Usul al-Fiqh*, p. 45.
31. Ibid., p. 46 ff.
32. Ibid., p. 49; Ibn al-Qayyim, *I'lam al-Muwaqq'in*, vol. I, p. 62.
33. Shalabi, *Al-Fiqh al-Islami*, pp. 147–148.
34. Abu Dawud, op.cit. vol. IV, p. 277, and Shawkani, op.cit. pp. 148–149.
35. Al-Mawardi, *Al-Ahkam al-Sultaniya*, p. 224; also see chapter 4 below on *ta'zir*.
36. Abu Dawud, op.cit., vol. IV, p. 277, and Shawkani, op.cit., p. 148, where Ahmad b. Hanbal is quoted.
37. Ibn al-Qayyim, *I'lam al-Muwaqq'in*, vol. II, p. 97; Shawkani, op.cit., p. 142; Ibn Farhun, *Tabsirah*, vol. II, p. 205; Shalabi, *Ta'lil al-Ahkam*, pp. 59–62.
38. Shalabi, op.cit.
39. *I'lam al-Muwaqq'in*, vol. II, p. 97.
40. Shawkani, *Nayl al-Awtar*, vol. VII, pp. 149-150, and *Mishkat al-Masabih*, vol. II,

p. 310. The words of the *hadith* are, "It is not allowed to give more than ten lashes, except for a *hadd* which pertains to Allah."

41. For this view, see Shawkani, op.cit., p. 147 ff.
42. *Muhalla,* vol. XI, pp. 365–370.
43. Qur'an, V:90 ff.
44. For the habit of drinking among Arabs, see *Ta'lil al-Ahkam,* p. 15.
45. Reuben Levy, *The Social Structure of Islam,* p. 346.
46. *Al-Mukhtar min al-Sihah,* p. 190.
47. See for example, Shafi'i, *Al-Umm,* vol. VII, p. 156. 'Uda, op.cit., vol. I, p. 79.
48. For example: II:217; III:90–91; and V:54.
49. XVI:106.
50. *Muhalla,* vol. XI, p. 195.
51. Suyuti, *Itqan,* vol. II, p. 22–24.
52. Heffening, *Encyclopaedia of Islam,* vol. III, p. 736 under *"Murtadd."*
53. See the preceding section dealing with punishment for *hiraba*.
54. See *Fath al-Bari,* vol. XII, p. 91, and Ibn Taymiyya, *Al-Sarim al-Maslul,* p. 319, for this view and p. 322 for its criticism.
55. Samuel Zwemre, *The Law of Apostasy in Islam,* pp. 39–40 and opposite p. 64, where the writer presents a photocopy of a page from Muslim's *Kitab al-Sahih* and comments on it; Goldziher, *Muslim Studies,* London, 1967, p. 16.
56. See Tabari, *Tafsir,* vol. VI, pp. 132–146; Ibn al-Qayyim, *Zad al-Ma'ad,* vol. III, p. 78; Ibn Hajar, *Fath al-Bari,* where he criticises Bukhari's view.
57. Bukhari, vol. XII, p. 169; Muslim, vol. XI, with the commentary of Nawawi, pp. 89–90; Abu Dawud, *Al-Sunan,* vol. IV, pp. 22–23.
58. See *Al-Sunan,* the commentaries on Bukhari, Muslim, and Abu Dawud.
59. Ibid., vol. IV, p. 223.
60. Ibn Taymiyya, *Al-Sarim al-Maslul,* pp. 315–396.
61. Bukhari, vol. XII, p. 228; Abu Dawud, vol. IV, p. 222; *Nayl al-Awtar,* vol. VII, pp. 190–191.
62. I have said "generally" because there is at least one jurist who views apostasy as merely a sin for which there is no *hadd* punishment, as will be seen later.
63. Muhammad 'Ali, *The Religion of Islam,* p. 596.
64. Ibid.
65. For details of his view, see Ibid., pp. 591–599.
66. *Muwatta',* with the commentary of al-Baji, vol. V, p. 281 ff.; *Nayl al-Awtar,* vol. VII, p. 193.
67. Sarakhsi, *Mabsut,* vol. X, pp. 108–110.
68. Examples of this may be found in any book of *fiqh,* e.g., *Minhaj al-Talibin,* vol. IV, pp. 123–132; Khirshi's commentary on *Mukhtasar Khalil,* vol. IV, pp. 304–316; and Shaikh 'Ali al-'Adawi's commentary in the margin of the same text.
69. Baydawi, *Minhaj al-Wusul, Ila 'Ilm al-Usul,* pp. 37–38; *Nasafi, Manar al-Anwar fi Usul al-Fiqh,* pp. 24–29; Khallaf, *Usul al-Fiqh,* pp. 194–195. Examples of these forms of usage may be found in the first authority.
70. *Nayl al-Awtar,* vol. VII, p. 192, where Shawkani indicates that all the reports according to which the Prophet killed an apostate are not trustworthy.
71. Bukhari, with the commentary of Ibn Hajar, vol. IV, p. 77, and vol. XIII, p. 170 Muslim with the comment of al-Nawawi, vol. IX, p. 391 ff.
72. Ibn Hajar, *Fath al-Bari;* also Nawawi's commentary on the text of Muslim, vol IX, p. 391, where he quotes Qadi 'Iyad, a well-known jurist, as saying that thi

bedouin was definitely an apostate. According to Zamakhshari, quoted in *Fath al-Bari*, the name of this bedouin is Qais ibn Hazim (probably al-Minqari).

73. Ibn Kathir, *Tafsir*, vol. 1, p. 373.
74. See n. 40 of chapter 4, p. 104.
75. See what was said above concerning the punishment for drinking.
76. *Nayl al-Awtar*, vol. VII, p. 191; Ibn Taymiyya, *Al-Sarim al-Maslul*, p. 320.
77. Ibn Taymiyya, op.cit., p. 318; *Mughni*, vol. VIII, p. 126; Shu'rani, *Mizan*, vol. II, p. 134.
78. Baji's commentary on *Al-Muwatta'*, vol. V, p. 282. Baji died 494 A.H.
79. Ibn Taymiyya, *Al-Siyasat al-Shar'iya*, p. 124.
80. See the *Encyclopaedia of Islam*, vol. II, p. 8927.
81. Sarakhsi, *Siyar*, vol. IV, p. 211; Shafi'i, *Umm*, vol. VI, p. 156.
82. *Mughni*, vol. VIII, p. 128.
83. See above, pp. 47-49.
84. 'Amer, *Al-Ta'zir*, p. 36.
85. See above, pp. 29-52.
86. Hall Williams, *The English Penal System in Transition*, 1970, pp. 11-13, and Thorsten Sellin's foreword to *Punishment and Social Structure*.
87. Page, op.cit., especially p. 83.
88. Muslim writers have treated these two crimes as being among the offences of *hudud*; hence what was said earlier about the inadequacy of their work (see p. 67) is applicable here.
89. G. M. Carstairs' foreword to Kessel and Walton's *Alcoholism*.
90. Ibid., p. 11.
91. Ibid., pp. 11-12.
92. II:219.
93. V:91.
94. Ibn al-Jawzi, *Zad al-Masir fi'Ilm al-Tafsir*, vol. II, p. 417.
95. Shalabi, *Ta'lil al-Ahkam*, pp. 15-17.
96. This right to make things lawful or unlawful was reserved to Allah in many Qur'anic verses, e.g., II:275; VI:119; VII:32-33; X:59, etc.
97. See, for example, what Ibn Kathir wrote concerning it in his *Tafsir al-Qur'an*, vol. I, p. 255.
98. Kessel and Walton, op.cit., pp. 30-42.
99. Frances Smart, *Neurosis and Crime*, pp. 24-25. See also Sir Norwood East, *Society and the Criminal*, pp. 281-293, and the Report of the Working Party on Habitual Drunken Offenders, London.
00. Smart, op.cit. pp. 15, 23 ff. and 168 ff.
01. First Ed., vol. I, chapts. 14 and 18, and vol. II, chap. 26.
02. Ibid., p. 248 and n. 40. The report was concerned with motor accidents in the U.K. and its results were published in *The Observer*, 6 Oct. 1959.
03. Ibid., pp. 248-249.
04. Fry, *Arms of the Law*, p. 189.
05. Mannheim, op.cit.
06. C. Hibbert, *The Roots of Evil*, pp. 255-259.
07. See, for example, 'Uda, op.cit., vol. I, p. 651.
08. See Honderich, op.cit., p. 176.
09. The explanatory memorandum of Articles 206 and 206 A, B and C of the penal code of Kuwait.
0. Although no figures are available concerning the effectiveness of the new punish-

ment in Kuwait, my own experiences there in the Legal Department of the Council of Ministers from 1967 to 1969 led to the stated conclusion.

111. Ibn Taymiyya, *Al-Siyasa al-Shar'iya'*, pp. 116–119. Qarafi, *Furuq*, vol. I, p. 216.
112. Articles 207 and 208.
113. See, for example, Ibn al-Qayyim, *Al-Turuq al-Hukmiya*, pp. 13, 100 ff; Mawdudi, *The Political Theory of Islam*, Arabic translation, pp. 49–51.
114. Al-Shatibi, *Al-I'tisam*, vol. II, pp. 244–245.
115. Ibn Hazm, *Al-Fisal fi al-Milal wa'al-Nihal*, vol. IV, pp. 171–176; 'Uda, *Al-Islam wa Awda'una al-Siyasiya*, pp. 151–153.
116. It was this principle which underlay the conflict led by some of the Shi'i leaders against the Ummayad and 'Abbassid States, behind the conflict between 'Ali b. Abi Talib and the Kharijites, and between the Wahhabis and the Ottoman Empire in the nineteenth century.
117. The outstanding example of this is the conflict between the Egyptian government and the Islamic movement known as the Society of the Muslim Brotherhood during the years 1954–65. For a brief but careful survey, see Hassan 'Ashmawi, one of the foremost leaders of the movement, in *Al-Fard al-'Arabi wa'Mushkilat al-Hukm* appended to his political play *Qalbun Akhr Li Ajl al-Za'im*, pp. 174–180.
118. 'Uda, op.cit., vol. I, pp. 534–538.
119. III:72.
120. See above, pp. 122–123.
121. Sarakhsi, *Mabsut*, vol. X, p. 110.
122. Muhammad 'Ali, op.cit., p. 599.
123. *Fath al-Qadir*, vol. IV, p. 389; Sarakhsi, op.cit.
124. See Mozley and Whiteley's *Law Dictionary*, under "Treason and Treason Felony," pp. 368–369. Also see the second book of the Egyptian penal code, Khalifa, *Al Nazariya' al-'Amma lil-Tajrim*, pp. 250–253.
125. The above view is concerned only with the penal sanction for apostasy; it does not affect the imposition of civil sanctions such as disinheritance and dissolution of marriage, etc.

CHAPTER III

Retaliation *(Alqisas)*: The Punishment For Homicide and Injuries

Undoubtedly the greatest crime known to mankind is murder. It has been punishable under all systems of law since early in the history of mankind and throughout the ages up to the present. The punishment prescribed in Islamic law for murder and the infliction of injury is what is called *"qisas"* or *"qawad"* (retaliation), that is inflicting on a culprit an injury exactly equal to the injury he inflicted on his victim.[1]

In studying the law of *qisas* in Islam, the most important point is the classification of the act of homicide; that is, is it a crime in which the state must intervene by means of punishment, or is it a civil wrong or tort, for which a remedy is available to the wronged individual if he so requests? The place given in Islamic law to the individual's wishes in the context of *qisas* distinguishes the Islamic treatment of homicide from its treatment under modern legal systems. For under Islamic law homicide appears to be essentially a civil wrong, the remedy for which is the concern of the victim or his relatives, rather than a crime in the strict sense. Such is one's first impression of the subject when one reads the Islamic law texts. But a close investigation may lead to a slightly different conclusion. We will return to this point later in the chapter. We will now consider the following points: the historical background of the law of *qisas* (retaliation) and *diya*(blood-money), some disputed points, and the application of *qisas* under the penal codes of some Muslim countries.

I. The Historical Background

A sense of hostility was a characteristic of the Arab tribesmen of pre-

69

Islamic Arabia; friendly co-operation in life was known only among the members of the same tribe.[2] One of the principal features of this state of hostility was personal revenge for homicide. The obligation of vengeance *(tha'r)* was inbred in the Arabs' very nature.[3] Historians often refer to cases of revenge between two or more tribes which began for a very trivial reason, such as the killing of a camel or an insulting word. Hostilities begun over such trifling reasons sometimes lasted for several years.[4] It was by no means rare for small disputes to turn into an actual war between two tribes; for example, the war between the tribes of Banu Bakr and Banu Taghlib lasted for forty years because one of the Bani Taghlib killed a female camel beloning to a woman of the Bani Bakr.[5] An attempt at a peace settlement was made after the son of a distinguished Arab, Shas b. Zuhayr b. Judhaymah, was killed, but the father asked the representative of the killer's tribe to do one of three things in order to stop him from taking revenge for his son: to return his son to life, to fill his garment *(rida)* with the stars, or to hand over to him all the members of the killer's tribe to be killed. "Still," the father added, "I will not be compensated for my son."[6]

One of the strongest causes behind the motive of revenge among Arab tribesmen was their belief that after the death of a murdered person a night-bird, known as *ham*, would stand on his grave and cry, "I am thirsty, give me a drink," that is, the revenge should take place to quench her thirst.[7] Moreover, revenge was taken not only against the murderer himself but against any of his fellow-tribesmen. Frequently tribal pride required several victims as equivalent to one fellow-tribesman, and the same was the case with regard to the infliction of injury.[8]

Blood-money *(diya)* was known among the Arab tribesmen as a peaceful alternative to revenge; but it varied according to the position of the murderer and his tribe. Among the Quraish the customary blood-money was a hundred camels, although for the nobles *(umara, s. amir)* it was one thousand. It was very common, on the other hand, for the blood-money of some tribes to be half that of other tribes, a rule which was due largely to the difference in strength and prestige between one tribe and another.[9]

Into this society Islam introduced the law of *qisas*. Just retaliation allowed one life, the life of the culprit himself, to be taken for the life of the murdered person, or a fixed amount of money to be exacted as blood-money. This was not to vary from one tribe to another or according to the victim's position in his tribe. We shall shortly discuss the law of *qisas* in detail, but at this stage we should note that the Qur'anic law "radically altered the legal incidents of homicide"[10] from the pre-Islamic custom of revenge (*tha'r*) to the Islamic law of *qisas*. The distinction is illustrated by the change of terminology. Justice is now to be measured "in accordance with the moral standard of just and exact reparation for loss suffered.'"[11] Moreover, the maxim "a life for a life " stems from the religious principle that all men are equal in the sight of God.[12] It was in terms of these principles that the exaction of *qisas* was prescribed, and it should be understood accordingly.

II. Retaliation and Blood-Money

The punishment for homicide and the infliction of injury in Islamic law could be either *qisas* (retaliation) or the payment of *diya* (blood-money). *Qisas* itself is divided into two categories: *qisas* for homicide (*fi'n-nafs*) and *qisas* for wounds or injuries (*fi'ma dum'an-nafs*). It is more common to use the term *qisas* for the former and the term *qawad* for the latter. As for *diya*, the term is commonly used to designate blood-money owed for killing, while the term *arash* is used for blood-money owed for injuries. Again, *diya* and *kaffara* (penance) are remedies for accidental homicide, but we will not deal with them at this stage as we are more concerned here with the punishment for deliberate homicide or injuries.

In the Qur'an both kinds of homicide, deliberate and accidental, are mentioned. For deliberate homicide the punishment prescribed in the Qur'an is the killing of the culprit or the payment of blood-money if the relative(s) of the victim do not demand *qisas*. The Qur'an enjoins: "O you who believe, retaliation is prescribed for you in the matter of the murdered; the freeman for the freeman, and the slave for the slave,[13] and the female for the female. But if any remission is made to him by his (injured) brother (in faith), then grant any reasonable demand and compensate him with handsome gratitude. This is an alleviation and a mercy from your Lord. And whoever transgresses after this, for him there will be a painful chastisement. In *qisas* there is life for you, O men of understanding, in order that you may restain yourselves.'"[14] And in another verse the law concerning accidental homicide is prescribed: "Never should a believer kill a believer unless by mistake. And whoever kills a believer by mistake should free a believing slave and pay compensation to the family of the deceased unless they remit it freely . . . ''[15] Taking these verses together, the jurists laid down the principle that no *qisas* is owed for accidental homicide but only the blood-money and penance, or *kaffara*.[16]

For deliberate homicide, the punishment of *qisas* means the taking of the culprit's life because of the life he has taken. This is, in modern terms, the death penalty for murder. The jurists are agreed on this, but their opinions vary concerning the means by which the death penalty should be carried out in cases of *qisas*.[17] The Hanafi and Hanbali schools hold that the culprit should be killed by the sword, whether or not he has killed his victim in this manner.[18] The Maliki, Shafi'i, and Zahiri schools, on the other hand, hold that the murderer should be put to death in the same manner in which he killed his victim.[19] The first view assumes that the purpose of prescribing *qisas* as a punishment is solely to put the murderer to death for his crime; hence he should be executed in the easiest and most efficient way.[20] The second view depends on an interpretation of the meaning of the word *qisas* as "equality;" accordingly, equality should be considered both in the taking of the cuplrit's life and in the means by which it is taken.[21]

According to the late Shaikh Shaltut, one should not concern oneself with the jurists' views about such a subject. It is related that the Prophet ordered the believers to improve the method of killing even for the slaughtering of animals; hence whatever quick, easy and efficient means of execution can be found should be used.[22] We may therefore conclude that retaliation for deliberate homicide is the punishment prescribed in the Qur'an, and that it should be carried out in the manner that causes the least possible pain.

Unlike retaliation for homicide, retaliation for injuries was not prescribed in clear terms either in the Qur'an or in the Sunna. The verses of the Qur'an on which the jurists based the law of retaliation for injuries are all controversial. The most important of them is verse 45, Surah V: "We prescribed for them (the Children of Israel) a life for a life, an eye for an eye, a nose for a nose, an ear for an ear, a tooth for a tooth, and for wounds retaliation . . . "[23] But to interpret this verse as the source of the law of retaliation for injuries is unjustified since it concerns what was revealed and prescribed for the Jews in the Torah. It is a part of a set of verses concerning the law prescribed for the Jews and the Christians; accordingly, it is not the proper verse on which to base a decision, particularly when the concluding part of this set of verses says: "For each of you (the prophets) we have appointed a divine law and a traced-out way,''[24] indicating the fact that every prophet has his own law revealed to him.[25]

The other verses which are used in the same manner are II:194 and XVI:126. Again, these verses are irrelevant in this context since they were revealed to regulate the relationship between Muslim and non-Muslim societies but not for governing the relationships of Muslim individuals with one another.[26]

As for the Sunna, there is only one report in which the Prophet is said to have ordered retaliation for injuries. This is the report transmitted by Bukhari and Muslim: a woman broke another woman's tooth and the Prophet ordered her tooth to be broken in retaliation, but her brother Anas b. al-Nadr swore that his sister's tooth could not be broken. Then the victim's relatives accepted *diya* instead of *qisas*.[27] Many points in this report have been subjects of discussion. Was it Anas b al-Nadr who swore that his sister's tooth could not be broken or was it his mother? Did this happen once or twice? The collectors of *hadith* are not unanimous about the Prophet's words, either. Moreover, the *hadith* rests only on "the information of one,"[28] which the scholars of *usul al-fiqh* deny to be a sound basis for establishing a law.[29]

Accordingly, one can say that the law of *qisas* for injuries is not laid down by the Qur'an or Sunna. Can we then find another source for it? According to Shaikh Shaltut it is based on consensus (*ijma'*); the jurists from the time of the Prophet until today are in agreement concerning it (although each school or individual jurist on a different basis). It is not a case of *ta'zir* which can either be adopted or not, but, according to all the schools of Islamic law, a law established on consensus which should be followed.[30]

The conditions required to apply *qisas* for injuries can be summarized as follows: (1) the injury must be deliberate (*'amd*) and not accidental (*khata*); (2) the part of the body on which *qisas* may be inflicted must be the same, and in the same condition, as the part of the victim's body which was injured by the culprit; and (3) *qisas* must be practicable to inflict, i.e., the injury must involve cutting off from a joint as, for example, from the wrist.[31] If all these conditions are fulfilled, *qisas* must be inflicted, according to Malik and Shafi'i, by experts in order that any possible error may be avoided.[32] The jurists of the Hanafi school hold that *qisas* for injuries should be inflicted in two cases only: the case of an injury which reaches the skull-bone (*al-muwaddaha*) and the case of articular injury (*al-jinaya 'ala-mifsal*).[33]

All other cases of injury are either unanimously held not to be subject to *qisas*, or agreed upon among the Hanafi jurists but not among others, or are subject to dispute among the Hanafi scholars themselves.[34] However, the texts of Islamic law contain quite lengthy discussions concerning the different kinds of injuries and the possibility of equality in retaliation for each, together with the possibility of fulfilling the other conditions required. All these discussions have been omitted here, since in my opinion it is a matter for expert and specific knowledge rather than for legal knowledge. One must accept the opinion of a surgeon, for example, about when just retaliation is physically possible and when it is not. A scholar of Islamic law has nothing to do with such a decision, as it is completely beyond his field of experience and knowledge. It is possible that the jurists may have made correct decisions concerning some of these matters, but in any case they cannot be taken as the final authority.[35]

It remains now to explain the other aspect of the punishment for homicide and wounding. *Diya* or blood-money is the sole punishment for quasi-deliberate homicide *(shabah al-'amd)*. It is due in cases of deliberate homicide if, and only if, the nearest relatives of the victim do not insist on the carrying-out of *qisas* against the murderer.[36] At the same time, *diya* (together with *kaffara*) is the penalty for accidental homicide. *Diya* as a remedy for homicide and injuries was described by the *Sunna* only. It is related that the Prophet said, "As for quasi-deliberate homicide *(shibhi al-'amd)*, the blood money is one hundred camels of which forty are pregnant."[37] In another report the same number of camels (one hundred) was fixed as the *diya* for deliberate homicide.[38]

Homicide is classified into categories which vary from one school to another, or even from one jurist to another within the same school. The largest number of classifications are those of the Hanafi school, which acknowledges five types: deliberate *('amd)*, quasi-deliberate *(shabah al-'amd)*, accidental *(khata')*, equivalent to accidental *(jari majra al-khata)* and indirect *(bisabab)*.[39] *Qisas* may be carried out for the first type of homicide only, while the penalty for the other four types is the exaction of blood-money.[40] These five classifications came into existence as the view of the Hanafi school after the famous Hanafi jurist al-Jassas (died 37 A.H.) wrote his book, *Ahkam al-Qur'an*. Before him, as he stated, the Hanafi jurists classified homicide into the first four categories only.[41] The Shafi'i, Hanbali, and Zaydi schools recognize only three classifications: deliberate, quasi-deliberate, and accidental, while the Maliki and Zahi schools divide homicide into two categories only: deliberate and accidental.[42]

The definition of each of these categories is disputed not only among different schools but also among different individual scholars of the same school. It is, as Professor Anderson rightly stated, a matter of "much complexity and confusion, for often the same writer will in places assert that deliberate homicide means homicide committed with the actual intention to kill, while in other places he will state or imply that it means homicide which results from an intentional use of any weapon or means intrinsically likely to kill."[43]

Whether or not the accused intended to kill another is something that only he can know. The difficulty of ascribing the intention to kill to the accused, in the absence of adequate proof, has led to a divergence of views among the schools of Islamic law as to the circumstances in which a homicide should be classified as deliberate. Generally speaking, the Hanafi, Shafi'i, and Hanbali schools classify as deliberate "cases of homicide in which the killer intended to kill and employed some means likely to have that result." Other cases of homicide which result from an act or omission which is not likely to kill are classified as quasi-deliberate homicide. The first category makes the offender liable only to *qisas*, while the second makes him liable to blood-money.[44]

The Maliki school, on the other hand, considers "a person guilty of deliberate homicide if he causes the death of another by any intentional act or omission directed against a human being, which is either hostile or intrinsically likely to kill."[45]

In cases of deliberate homicide, the punishment is the death penalty by means of *qisas*. However, *qisas* may be ruled out if the victims' nearest relatives do not demand it or, in other cases, if it is impossible to carry it out.[46] The relatives may then ask for the payment of *diya* or forgive the killer altogether. Whenever they insist upon the payment of *diya*, it is to be in the value of one hundred camels, and the same *diya* is due in all cases of quasi-deliberate homicide, as this does not incur *qisas* (here again the relatives are free to forgive the killer).[47] Accordingly, *diya* is the only punishment in cases of quasi-deliberate homicide, and it is also a substitute punishment in cases of deliberate homicide. In both cases it is to be one hundred camels,[48] according to one view, on the heavier or higher scale, and, according to the other, on the ordinary or lighter scale. The same dispute exists concerning quasi-deliberate and deliberate homicide.[49] Although the *diya* was originally fixed in terms of camels, it is almost universally admitted that it can be paid by an equivalent amount of money, either gold or silver, cows, sheep or garments. As for the Zahiri school, it holds that it should be paid only in camels unless this is impossible, there being no camels available, in which case it can be paid by the price equivalent to one hundred camels.[50]

In cases of deliberate homicide, the culprit himself is to pay the *diya* from his own property. However, there are various opinions among the schools concerning deliberate homicide committed by an insane man or a minor *(saghir)*. Apart from the prevailing view of the Shafi'is, the three schools agree that the *diya* in such a case is to be paid by the *aqila* (tribal group to which the culprit belongs). This is based on the fact that both a minor and an insane person possess a defective power of discrimination with regard to values and behavior. Moreover, Islamic law is not regarded as applicable to those who have not reached puberty or who are insane.[51] The Shafi'is' prevalent view allows the *diya* to be paid from the insane or minor person's property by method of analogical reasoning *(qiyas)*, on the grounds that they are subject to *ta'zir* for their actions.[52]

In cases of quasi-deliberate homicide, the *diya* is to be paid by the '*aqila* of the culprit, according to all the schools except the Maliki, which does not recognize quasi-deliberate homicide (nor does the Zahiri school, of course).[53] An important difference between the payment of *diya* in deliberate and quasi-deliberate homicide is that in the former it is to be paid immediately after the case is closed by the court, while in the latter it is to be paid within three years, starting either from the day of the victim's death (according to the Shafi'i and Hanbali schools), or from the day on which the case was closed by the court (according to the Hanafi view).[54] There are indeed many points of dispute and contradictory opinions, but we need not go into these here.[55] Among the points of universal agreement in Islamic law is that the blood-money of a woman is half that of a man.[56] It is interesting, however, that all jurists are agreed that it is allowed to the nearest relative of the victim and the culprit to settle the matter peacefully *(sulhan)* on the supposition that the culprit may pay the victim's relatives more money than the amount fixed for *diya*.[57]

Thus far we have summarized the principles of the law of *diya* for homicide, and it now remains for us to consider the law of *diya* for injuries or wounds. This subject, in the texts of Islamic law, is very complex and confusing. Nearly every part of the human body has been considered in relation to the amount of *diya* or *arash* which is due to be paid for its injury, and most of the related points were disputed. Because we are not con-

:erned here with explaining the law but with stating its general principles in order to understand the rationale for the punishments prescribed for crimes, we will not go into these disputed points at all. It is sufficient to state that for some injuries, e.g., the eyes, nose, lips, etc., the full amount of *diya* is due, while for others a fixed amount, or percentage of it, should be paid (although there are differing views concerning various injuries as well). If there is no fixed amount in terms of either the whole or part of the *diya*, the victim is entitled to a compensation known as *hukumat 'adl*. This is an amount of money to be fixed by the judge (*qadi*) and paid to the victim for the loss suffered. The fixed amounts are to be assessed either from what the Prophet reportedly laid down in his letter to 'Amr b. Hazm when he was appointed to represent the Prophet in Yemen,[58] or from personal opinion *(ijtihad)*.[59]

All jurists agree that the blood-money (*diya* or *arash)* may replace retaliation when it is not possible to inflict it or when a peaceful agreement *(sulh)* is achieved.[60] According to some jurists, blood-money is also due if the culprit has already lost that part of his body corresponding to the part of the victim's body which he injured, while according to other jurists nothing is due in such a case.[61] The payment of *diya* in cases of injury is the duty of the culprit himself; here the *'aqila* is exempt from any responsibility, as the deed is the culprit's alone and so should be the compensation due for it. On this point, complete agreement has been established among all the schools of Islamic law.[62]

III. Disputed Points Concerning the Infliction of *Qisas*

Under this heading we shall consider three points: the execution of *qisas* against a group of people for killing a single person, against a Muslim for killing a non-Muslim *(dhimmi),* and against a father for killing his son. Although many other disputed points are treated in the texts of Islamic law, these are the most important ones since they are directly concerned with the fundamental principle of *qisas* itself.

Qisas was prescribed to combat the desire to kill in man's nature. "In qisas there is life for you,"[63] is the obvious reason given by the Qur'an for legalizing this punishment. To hold the view that in the above-mentioned cases *qisas* cannot be inflicted is to demolish the theory of *qisas* itself. Accordingly, we will attempt here to see what evidence supports such a view and to what extent it can be accepted.

III. 1   *Qisas* Against a Group for the Killing of a Single Person

Murder can be committed by one person or by a group of people against one person. In the first case there is no problem about inflicting *qisas* on the culprit, but in the second some Muslim jurists hold that while a man should be executed for killing one man, a group should not. This view was reportedly held by Zuhari Ibn Sirin, and Habib b. Abi Thabit, among others. The Hanafi, Maliki, Shafi'i, and Zahiri schools hold an opposite view, according to which a group can be punished by means of *qisas* for killing one person. It is not clear, however, which view was held by Ibn 'Abbas and Ahmad b. Hanbal since both views were attributed to both of them.[64]

Those who hold the first view support it by an interpretation of the two Qur'anic verses in Surahs II and V in which it is mentioned that one person may be killed for one person. Accordingly, they claim, two or more people are not "equal" to one, and as the law of *qisas* is based on "equality," it is not justifiable to kill more than one person for killing a single individual.

In fact, it is easy to refute this claim by saying that *qisas* is a punishment for a specific act, i.e., the killing of a person, and any punishment can be inflicted for the commission of the act for which it was prescribed regardless of the number of people who shared in it. Thus, when four people shared in killing a boy in Yemen, 'Omar ordered his representative there to carry out *qisas* against them; the same was done by 'Ali when three men killed a single man.[65] Moreover, if the first view were correct it would open the door to anyone who wants to kill a person by allowing him to seek the cooperation of a third individual and thus escape punishment.[66] Accordingly, the preferable view in relation to this point is the majority one which allows *qisas* to be inflicted upon a group of people for killing one person. The same applies to cases of executing *qisas* against a man for killing a woman.

III. 2   *Qisas* Against a Muslim for Killing a Non-Muslim

It is characteristic in religious laws to consider the followers of the religion in question superior to others who do not profess this religion. This distinction is clearly expressed in the Qur'an and the Sunna in relation to the position of people in the sight of God, especially in the hereafter.[67] According to this distinction, the majority of Muslim scholars hold that a Muslim is not liable to *qisas* if he has killed a non-Muslim *(dhimmi)*.[68] Only the Hanafi school holds that *qisas* is to take place in such a case.[69]

This majority view is supported by Qur'anic verses which declare that non-Muslims are not equal to Muslims and by a *hadith* which forbade the killing of a Muslim on account of his killing a non-Muslim *(kafir)*.[70] At the same time the Hanafi school supports its view by insisting on the application of the general meaning of the Qur'anic verses relating to *qisas* which do not discriminate between a Muslim and a non-Muslim but simply declare *qisas* to be the punishment for homicide disregarding the faith of the victim.[71] One can add to this the *hadith* reported by Bukhari, Muslim, and Dawud: "The life of a Muslim may be taken in three cases only — i.e., in the case of a married person who commits *zina,* one who has killed a human being *(qutal nafsan),* and one who has forsaken his religion and separated himself from his community.' "[72] Here, as we see, the victim of the act is described as "a human being" in general and not simply as a Muslim human being.

Moreover, to limit the infliction of *qisas* only to cases involving the killing of a Muslim is contradictory to the principle of the law of *qisas* itself, as was stated before. This law was made in order to protect human life, and if one imposes such a limitation on it, it is a clear contradiction of its purpose. One cannot deny that the law of *qisas* is based on equality, but equality in what? This is the question. The Hanafi school rightly holds that equality here means that both the killer and the victim must be human beings; therefore, any human being who kills another human being is liable to *qisas* disregarding the religion of the victim. The Qur'anic verses cited by other schools to support their view that there is no equality between a Muslim and a non-Muslim all relate to the Hereafter, and hence none of them is relevant to this discussion.[73]

As for the *hadith* concerned, its words are not clear concerning the verdict intended by the Prophet; consequently, an explanation was neccessary. It is obvious from what Jassas said about it that the explanation given by the Hanafi school is harmonious with the general spirit of Islamic law rather than with the explanation given by the majority.[74] It may be said here that the Hanafis' view, and that of the Malikis in cases of deceit *(ghila),* assumes that *qisas* is a punishment by the authority for the sake of justice. The majority view, on the other hand, is influenced by the pre-Islamic distinction between individuals according to their social or tribal position, a distinction which Islam condemned. On this basis, contemporary scholars are generally in favor of the Hanafis' view rather than that of the majority.[75]

At the same time a parallel may be drawn between the Hanafis' view and the view unanimously agreed upon concerning theft. There is a complete consensus concerning the fact that if a Muslim steals a non-Muslim's property and the crime is proved, the Muslim's hand is to be amputated; the cause or *'illa* of this is the protection of the non-Muslim's property. It is clear enough how illogical it would be to grant more protection to the property of a non-Muslim than his life.[76] This view may be objected to on the grounds that the punishment for theft is owed to God *(haqq Allah)* and therefore it cannot be equal to *qisas* as the latter is essentially due to the victim or his relatives, i.e., *haqq adami.* Such an objection is not valid. This parallel does not affect the fact that while the punishment for theft pertains to *haqq Allah*, it has the clear object of prescribing a punishment for theft, i.e., the protection of property.[77]

III. 3. Qisas *Against a Father for Killing His Son*

Two views are held by Muslim jurists concerning this point. The Hanafi, Shafi'i and Hanbali schools hold that a father who kills his son is not liable to *qisas*, while the Maliki school hold an opposite view, according to which the father is liable to *qisas* for killing his son if the homicide is proved.

The three schools' views are based on many arguments. First there is the alleged *hadith* stating, "No retaliation is due in cases of a father who kills his son." Second, it is maintained that *qisas* is prescribed to prevent the commission of homicide, and the love of the father for his son would prevent him from such an act. Third, it is claimed that since the father is the direct cause of his son's being alive, it is not right that the son should become the cause of his father's death.[80]

To consider this evidence, it is clear that the second and the third arguments are not based on any legal principle but are emotional statements which have nothing to do with a legal topic. The third piece of evidence is in fact a falsification, for in such a case it is not true that the son is the cause of his father's death; it is the father's own deed which results in his death. The son was the father's victim, and the father is merely facing his rightful punishment in being subject to *qisas*.[81] As for the *hadith* cited, it is sufficient to state that since at least three scholars of *hadith* have declared it to be related by untrustworthy people, such a *hadith* cannot be used as evidence to prove or to refute any legal view.[82]

The Maliki view is supported by the general import of the Qur'anic verses, which do not distinguish one killer from another or one victim from another. Again this view is supported by all the contemporary writers concerning the subject, as it is in harmony with the Islamic legal principles of equality as applied in the law of *qisas*.[83] It is clear that the Maliki view conforms to the principle of punishment administered by the state for the sake of justice, which allows no distinction between offenders based on their relationship to the victim. The majority view, on the other hand, considers homicide as a civil offence for which, according to another *hadith,* no redress is granted to the son against his father.[84] A final note concerning all these disputed points is that the opinion held concerning each of them is applicable to cases of *qisas* for wounding as well.

IV. The Application of *Qisas* in Muslim Countries

We shall concern ourselves with considering the possibility of applying the law of *qisas* in Egypt under the current penal code. This matter has been discussed in relation to the explanation of the first article of the Egyptian penal code of 1883. A reservation was made in this article that no interference with the personal rights granted according to Islamic law, the *Shari'a*, should result from the adoption of the penal code. Soon after the adoption of the code, a case known as the case of Fyruz Agha initiated the conflict between the law of *qisas* and the punishment prescribed in this code for homicide. The culprit's defendant claimed that the prosecutor had no right to demand the infliction of the death penalty as this demand is the "right of the relatives of the victim according to the *Shari'a.*"[85] The court rejected this claim, explaining that the reservation in the first article referred only to *diya*, while punishment was entirely a "government task." This view was approved by the court of appeal on September 8, 1889.[86]

The commentators afterwards discussed the problem; they were divided into three groups. The first held the view that the punishments prescribed in this code for homicide and wounding abrogated the law of *qisas*, but they allowed, on the basis of the reservation mentioned in Article 1, the right of the injured party to claim *diya*.[87] The second held the view that although *qisas* was still a part of the penal law according to the above-mentioned article, a court would not administer it as it contradicted the principles of modern penal law which were introduced into the Egyptian penal code of 1883. Such a decision would be against the law, and accordingly this reservation should be abolished.[88]

The Egyptian penal code was amended in 1937, but this clause was reintroduced in Article 7 of the new code. Dr. Ahmad Ibrahim, in his thesis entitled *Al-Qisas*, defended a third view, according to which the law of *qisas* was held to be a part of the Egyptian penal law, which the court should adopt where all the conditions laid down by the *Shari'a* are fulfilled.[89] According to his view, a crime of homicide or wounding has two punishments determined by the law: (1) the punishment of *qisas* as laid down in the *Shari'a* and (2) the punishment prescribed in the penal code. A conflict between the two punishments could be resolved on the basis of Article 32 of the 1937 penal code, which allows only the more severe punishment to be inflicted in such a case.[90] Although the evidence put forth by Dr. Ibrahim is theoretically quite sound, in practice his view cannot be accepted for many reasons. The most important question concerns which *madhhab* or school of Islamic law the court should take as its model.

We have seen some of the disputed points among the schools, and there are many more. In a modern state, it is the legislator who must decide which school or opinion should be followed. It should not be forgotten that this difficulty was the reason behind recent legislation on inheritance and legacy in most Muslim countries, and the situation is likely to be even more intolerable concerning the law of *qisas*. Moreover, a realistic view concerning the clause of Article 1 of the 1883 code and Article 7 of the 1937 code is that both articles were introduced into the respective codes to satisfy the popular belief that the *Shari'a* is the basic law of the country, and accordingly it should not be overruled by any legislation; this was merely a pretence since it is clear that none of the *shari'a* punishments were enforced by these codes. Evidence for this is that no one except Dr. Ibrahim himself expressed or supported his view, and, as far as I know, the criminal courts have never faced the problem of adopting the law of *qisas* since the case of Fyruz Agha in 1889.

If the law of *qisas* is to be adopted in Egypt, or in any Muslim country, it should be implemented through a piece of legislation in order to void the difficulties expected from its adoption, according to Dr. brahim's view. But insofar as the circumstances remain the same, this is ery unlikely to occur. On the contrary, some writers are convinced that the eservation in Article 7 of the current penal code in Egypt is on the way toward eing abolished in the new penal code now in preparation. It was made, as has een said, for a particular reason which no longer really exists; it is therefore eaningless to retain it.[91]

√. The Classification of Homicide

At the very beginning of his article, "Homicide in Islamic Law,"[92] Professor Anderson draws attention to the fact that in the text books of slamic law homicide is treated as a tort rather than as a crime. Accordngly, the question of the classification of homicide between these two ategories will be considered here.[92]

It may be helpful to begin with a definition of both tort and crime n order to clarify the subject, and then to see whether Islamic law treats omicide as a tort, a crime, or both at the same time. Indeed, the matter f defining both tort and crime is far from being settled, but we need not dd anything to the current arguments on the subject. Rather it is preferale to take one of the many definitions provided by the authorities on each ubject as the basis for this study.

As for tort, the best definition known in English law for tortious liabilty is that of Winfield: "Tortious liability arises from the breach of a duty rimarily fixed by the law; this duty is towards persons generally and its reach is redressable by an action for unliquidated damages."[93] Tortious iability is distinguishable from criminal liability by the fact that a crime is 'a wrong the sanction of which involves punishment.'[94] Again, we can lefine criminal prosecution as concerned with the imposition of penalties pon the wrong-doer in order to protect society as a whole, while "tort iability, on the other hand, exists primarily to compensate the person inured by compelling the wrong-doer to pay for the damage he has lone."[95]

According to these definitions, one can say that the distinction beween a tort and a crime, generally speaking, appears in the purpose unlerlying the court's decision. If it is to compensate the injured party, then t is a case of tort. On the other hand, if it is to punish the wrong-doer, it s a criminal case. The wronged party has nothing to do with the trial or the carrying out of the court's decision in the latter case, while in the former, he will benefit from its decision by the compensation payable to him or the repair of his damaged property.[96]

Now to turn to homicide in Islamic law, the victim or his nearest relatives have three rights: first, the right to demand the execution of *qisas* against the murderer; second, the right to pardon the murderer in return for his paying the fixed amount of blood-money; and, third, the right to pardon him freely, i.e., even without taking the blood-money. Here these three rights will be considered in turn in order to reach the correct classification of homicide.

It is the right of the nearest relative of the murdered person to demand retaliation or *qisas,* and without this demand *qisas* cannot be inflicted. The jurists have added to this that when *qisas* is demanded, it is the right of the relatives of the murdered person to carry it out, and they should not be deprived of this right, if they are capable of doing so in the proper way.[97] This is the view of the four Sunni schools, and it is clear that the old tradition of personal revenge was the reason behind this view.[98] This view, moreover, was supported by an interpretation of the Qur'anic verse ". . .and if anyone is slain wrongfully, we have given his heir authority . . ." (XVII:33).

To explain this "authority" which pertains to the heir, the majority hold that it is the authority to kill the culprit. On the other hand, some of the commentators on the Qur'an explain it as the heir's right to demand the execution of *qisas* or to remit it. But the execution itself is the state's responsibility and not anyone else's.[99]

In the majority view, *qisas* is clearly a matter of private justice, or rather personal vengeance, but in the other view the idea of crime and punishment emerges. This view is held by all the contemporary writers on the subject.[100] The strongest evidence used to support this view is that in the Qur'an *qisas* is described as the duty of the Muslim community, which cannot carry it out except through a representative, who would be, in this case, the judge or ruler. To explain this concept, Shaltut states that the duties of the community in Islam are two-fold. First, there are the duties obligatory for each individual, such as prayer, fasting and the payment of *zakat;* second, there are those carried out by a representative acting on behalf of the community, since it is impossible for each Muslim to perform them individually. One of these duties is the carrying out of qisas when it is demanded.[101]

As for the second right of the victim's relatives, i.e., the right to rem retaliation and to receive the *diya*, it is here that homicide appears to be more of a tort rather than a crime. The *diya* is, above all, a compensation, fixed to satisfy the victim's relatives. This is even more clear in cases where the matter is settled out of court for an amount greater or smaller than the fixed *diya*. If it is argued that in cases in which the court orders the payment of *diya*, that such payment constitutes a kind of punishment, such an argument is completely unfounded in the latter case.

Moreover, the victim's relatives have the right to remit retaliation freely, without any compensation being given. This right may be exercised even after the court has ordered *qisas* to be executed against the culprit. And indeed, the Qur'an and the Sunna recommend the remission of retaliation.[102] To use Professor Anderson's words, "It is regarded as more meritorious to remit retaliation, and for this reason most jurists hold that if any adult, sane heir waives this right, the others have no option but to comply."[103] According to most of the jurists, if the right of remission is exercised, the culprit is not liable to any punishment. However, the Maliki school allows a discretionary punishment (*ta'zir*) to be inflicted in this case, and indeed in all cases of deliberate homicide in which, for one reason or another, there has been no retaliation.[104] In the Maliki view, crime is seen as that which should be punished for the sake of justice itself.[105]

It can be said, therefore, that neither the concept of crime nor that of tort is
It can be said, therefore, that neither the concept of crime nor of tort is dominant. Consequently, one may rightly conclude that homicide and its punishment in Islamic law have a dual nature, that of a crime for which punishment is imposed and that of a tort which makes the wrongdoer liable to pay a compensation from which the wronged party may benefit. Of course, such a dual system with regard to homicide is completely divorced from the modern idea of crime and punishment; it is the heritage of the ancient pre-Islamic Arab tradition which was modified by Islamic law and by no means comlpletely changed.[106] Indeed, the concept of punishment inflicted by the state for homicide was, as far as the Arabs were concerned, an innovation of Islam, but this does not mean that there was a complete change-over from the pre-Islamic conception.

VI. A Survey of the Law of *Qisas*

Several points need to be discussed in this part of the study. Perhaps the first one of interest is that of *qisas*.

It is said in the Qur'an that *qisas* was prescribed for the Jews in the Torah. This fact can be seen in the Torah itself, where nearly the same words are used as in the Qur'an. In the Old Testament one of the Ten Commandments is, "Thou shalt not kill," and the punishment for disobeying it came shortly after it: "Whoever strikes a man so that he dies shall be put to death."[107] The commandment not to kill and the punishment for killing were both revealed again in the Qur'an in almost the same words.[108]

Again, the detailed law of *qisas* for injuries which was laid down in the Qur'an V:45 is also found in the Old Testament: "A life for a life, an eye for an eye, a tooth for a tooth, a hand for a hand, a foot for a foot, a burn for a burn, a wound for a wound."[109] The rule that gives the nearest relative of the victim the right to ask for the punishment of the culprit, or even to carry it out himself, is also prescribed in the Torah.[110]

According to some Muslim commentators, the law of retaliation was omitted from the New Testament. This view is supported by what is written in Matthew: "You have heard that it was said, 'An eye for an eye and a tooth for a tooth.' But I say to you, do not resist one who is evil. But if any one strikes you on the right cheek, turn to him the other also.'"[111] But these New Testament verses should be interpreted in the light of another statement of Jesus: "Think not that I have come to abolish the law and the Prophets; I have come not to abolish them but to fulfil them."[112]

The law of retaliation was undoubtedly a part of the law of Moses which Jesus came to fulfil. Its fulfilment in this context was accomplished by adding to the concrete law of retaliation laid down by Moses in the Torah the command of forgiveness and mercy. The command to forgive was later revealed again in the Qur'an, and it cannot be said that it contains any contradiction to the law of *qisas*.[113] In accordance with this, it becomes clear that Islam did not initiate this law. All three of the world's major religions approve the law of *qisas* as a part of their ordinances for the control of human behavior. *Qisas* was known before Islam to the followers of Judaism and Christianity, and its introduction into Islam was a reassertion that it is God's law which must be obeyed.

However, we have here to consider the law of *qisas* in the light of modern penologists' theories and ideas. It has been mentioned above that *qisas* for homicide means inflicting the death penalty as a punishment for the crime, whereas *qisas* for injuries, when it can be applied, means a corporal punishment. The notion of *diya*, or blood-money, may be compared with the modern concept of compensation to the victim or the wronged party.

To begin with capital punishment, it is well-known that the arguments for and against it have been in existence for a long time. Most European countries have not abolished it; the last country to do so was England. The Abolition of the Death Penalty Act of 1965 abolished capital punishment as a punishment for murder, although it can still be inflicted for treason and piracy with violence. Until 1971 it was also the punishment for setting fire to H.M. ships and dockyards, but the 1971 Criminal Damage Act subsequently abolished it for these offenses, which are now punishable by life imprisonment (See 11, 1 and 2, and Sec. 4, 1). However, the possibility of applying capital punishment seems to be, under the present circumstances, much more theoretical than practical.

In other parts of the world including the United States and the Arab countries, capital punishment is the penalty for murder. In the United States, generally speaking, it can be enforced for deliberate murder which falls within the category of "murder in the first degree,"[114] and in the Arab countries for murder committed deliberately. If the argument has ended in England and most European countries in favor of the "abolitionists," it is still continuing in other countries on almost the same grounds as in the countries which have abolished it. A brief account of the relevant evidence may be sufficient here.[115]

In the first place, those who defend the abolition of the death penalty support their argument by the fact that its abolition in other countries has proved to be successful. There are also other objections to the punishment itself, such as "the irrevocability of the death sentence, and the consequent danger of the execution of an innocent person, . . .the depressing, and indeed demoralising, effect of execution upon both the officers of the prison and other prisoners; the false glamour which the existence of the death penalty throws over murder trials."[116]

The supporters of the death penalty, on the other hand, often argue along the same lines as Leo Page, that

these arguments are erroneous. Law exists for the protection of the community. It is not necessary to show that capital punishment is an absolute preventative of murder, or even that it is the only deterrent. If it can be shown that it is more effective as a deterrent than any other punishment, then I shall be satisfied that it should be retained. To hold otherwise is surely to forget the innocent victims of murder in the interests of their murderers. And I have no doubt at all that the fear of the gallows is the most powerful of all deterrents.[117]

As for the other points, Page states: "The most searching examination of records for the past fifty years (up to 1937) has failed to bring to light a single case in which it can be suggested that an innocent person has been hanged."[118] Experts in prison administration are usually quoted as supporters of capital punishment, and great stress is laid on this by Page, as well as on the fact that social circumstances differ from one country to another. Hence, what may justify abolition in one may not be at all relevant in another.[119]

The deterrent effect of capital punishment has been discussed a great deal, and it has often been suggested that life imprisonment would be a similar, if not a better, deterrent.[120] But as far as the English penal system is concerned, life imprisonment means from ten to fifteen years imprisonment. The Home Secretary announced on 22 April 1970 that 172 convicted murderers had been released from prison since 1960, most of them having served nine years or less of their statutory life sentence. Only five of this number had served twelve years or more, while nine had served six years or less, and one had completed only six months. In a written answer to a Parliamentary question, the Secretary of State for the Home Department announced figures concerning life sentences up to 2 November 1972. These figures show that the average period served as life imprisonment in 1971 was 10.5. years, while the longest average in the past ten years was 8.9. years (1964 and 1968) and the shortest average was 7.7 years (1961 and 1963)[121] In light of these statistics, life imprisonment is surely questionable as an effective deterrent to serious crime.

As far as the Arab countries are concerned, the arguments on this subject were imported from the West. There are two main trends of opinion, one for abolition and one for retention of the death penalty, as well as a compromise position which holds that it must be abolished in general but retained for some serious offenses and for political crimes.[122]

To turn to corporal punishment, it must be noted that it has been abolished in most countries for a relatively long time. Even in the Arab countries, where it is considered part of the religious law of Islam, it was abolished almost everywhere early in the twentieth century. In some countries corporal punishment was reintroduced in wartime as a punishment for some crimes, but since then it has been abolished. An exception to this abolition is for crimes committed in prisons and by members of the national force during their service.[123]

We need not discuss here the different views on corporal punishment since such a discussion would have no practical value. From the theoretical point of view, all that is said about capital punishment may be applied to corporal punishment as well. The topic has been fully discussed, however, in the *Report o the Departmental Committee on Corporal Punishment* in England, 1938. The Committee's unanimous opinion at the end of their inquiry was that "corporal punishment was of no special value as a deterrent and should be abolished."[124] Once again, the diversity of views about corporal punishment was imported into the Arab countries, but the different positions were of lesser import than those relating to capital punishment.[125]

As we have seen, the alternative punishment for homicide or injuries in Islamic law is blood-money, or *diya* for homicide and *arash* for wounding. It has been seen that the *diya* or *arash* must be paid to the victim in cases of injury and to his nearest relative(s) in cases of homicide. According to 'Uda, *diya* is a compensation to the victim and his relatives, as well as a punishment inflicted upon the culprit. He argues that it is a punishment because it is determined by the law, and when the victim or his relative(s) remit retaliation freely without taking *diya,* the culprit may be subject to a discretionary punishment (*ta'zir*).[126] But this view may be objected to as its evidence is not, as claimed, the concrete law on the subject. The amount of *diya* determined was seen earlier to be by no means mandatory. The parties concerned may agree to settle the matter for more, or even for less, than the amount determined for the case. The discretionary punishment is not universally agreed upon, either. Some jurists allow it to be implosed while others do not, or at least have not expressed their view in relation to it.

Accordingly, the preferable view concerning *diya* may be that it is an institution established in order to satisfy the victim or his relatives by compensating them for the harm suffered. It may have some penal function similar to that of punishment, but that is only an incidental or secondary function. The idea of compensation to those who have suffered harm or damage is well-established in Western legal systems as part of the law of civil procedure.[127]

As for criminal procedure, a compensatory system is not yet common in Western countries. This idea was discussed in relation to victims of crimes of violence in England and Wales in two reports submitted to the House of Commons in 1961 and 1964, but has not yet entered current legislation (see below).[128] The discussion in the two reports concentrated on the idea that the state may pay the proposed compensation in order to help those who were affected by a crime of violence.

It is here that we see the difference between the concept of compensation as introduced in Western thought and as it is known in Islamic law. Although it has been suggested that in Muslim countries the state must take the responsibility for paying the *diya* or blood-money in cases where the culprit cannot afford it, it is still primarily the culprit's responsibility. In the above-mentioned reports it is proposed as a social duty to be carried out by the state.[129]

It is interesting, however, that the 1971 Criminal Justice Bill contains a section dealing with compensation orders against convicted persons. Under this Bill, it is proposed that a court may order the offender to pay compensation in respect of any personal injury or any loss of, or damage to, property caused by the offence for which he was tried before the court or any offense which was taken into consideration by it. If this Bill receives the approval of Parliament, the compensation order for personal injury may be rightly compared with the rules of *diya* and *arash* in Islamic law. In the meantime, since March 1964, a non-statutory scheme, administered by the Victims of Crimes of Violence Compensation Board, is in effect in England. The Board consists of a committee of eight experienced lawyers (originally five), together with a lawyer as a chairman, who deal with the applications for compensation and make decisions concerning the awards. The awards are to be paid by the state and not the offender. An amended scheme was adopted in May 1969 and is reprinted in the fifth Report of the Work of the Board. In 1964 the Government of New Zealand also introduced a statutory scheme of compensation, and since then several American states have followed suit.[130]

NOTES

1. The word *qisas* is derived from the verb *qassa*, meaning "he cut" or "he followed his track in pursuit;" hence it came to mean retaliation by killing for killing, or injuries for injuries. The word *qawad* is derived from the verb *qada*, meaning "to drive" or "to lead." Its usage in the definition of *qisas* is due to the fact that the culprit was often led by something (e.g., a piece of rope) to the place of execution or because he was led by his action to the result which followed, i.e., the carrying out of *qisas* against him. However, the word *qisas* is much more common in Islamic legal writing than the word *qawad*. For details see Ibn Manzur, *Lisan al-'Arab* vol. VIII, p. 341; Ibn Faris, *Mu'jam Maqayis al-Lughat*, vol. V, p. 11; Sharabasi *Al-Qisas fil-Islam*, p. 17.
2. Ahmad Ibrahim, *Al-Qisas fil-Shari'a al-Islamiya*, p. 9. It is noteworthy that the Qur'an mentions this fact in more than one verse in different Surahs, e.g., III:10 and VIII:63.

3. Anderson, Homicide in Islamic Law, *Bull. of the School of Oriental and African Studies*, 1951, p. 811.
4. Ibn 'Abd-Rabbih, *Al-'Iqd al-Farid*, vol. VI, pp. 40, 71–77.
5. Kulayb b. Rabi'a killed a female camel belonging to al-Basus bint Munqidh. See ibid., pp. 40, 71-77.
6. Shafi'i, *Umm*, vol. VI, p. 7.
7. Damiri, *Hayat al-Hayawan*, vol. II, pp. 437–440; al-Jahiz, *Kitab al-Hayawan* ,vol. II, p. 298.
8. Ibrahim, op. cit., p. 9; Anderson, op. cit., p. 812.
9. Ibrahim, op. cit., p. 10; Ibn Kathir, *Tafsir*, vol. I, p. 209.
10. Coulson, *A History of Islamic Law*, p. 18.
11. Ibid., p. 18.
12. Coulson, *op. cit.* It is noteworthy that Prof. Coulson here confirms the majority's view which claims equality among Muslims but not between them and non-Muslims. But according to the Hanafi school, equality in relation to this particular question is based not on religion but on being a human being; hence, *qisas* is to be implemented when a Muslim kills a non-Muslim, although the view of the majority does not allow *qisas* in this case but only the payment blood-money.
13. Here, and throughout this work, I am omitting everything that is found in the books of *fiqh* concerning slaves, simply because this has long been a matter of historical concern only.
14. II:178–179.
15. IV:92.
16. Jassas, *Ahkam al-Qur'an*, vol. II, p. 222 ff.; Shafi'i, *Umm*, vol. VI, p. 4 ff.
17. For reasons of clarity, I prefer to discuss this point here rather than to add it to other controversial points which we will discuss later.
18. Jassas, op. cit., vol. I, pp. 160-161; *Suyuty Matalib uli al-Nuha, Sharh Ghayat al-Muntaha, vol. VI, p. 52.*
19. *Mudawwanah*, vol. IV, pp. 495–496; *Umm*, vol. VI, p. 54; *Muhalla*, vol. X, pp. 370-373.
20. Jassas, op. cit., p. 161; *Matalib uli al-Nuha*, p. 52.
21. *Muhalla*, p. 370 ff.; Jassas, op. cit.
22. Mahmud Shaltut, *Islam 'Aqida wa-Shari'a*, p. 383. See also a decision *(fatwa)* of the Azhar jurists' committee, *Majallt al-Azhar*, vol. VIII, p. 503, referred to in Ibrahim's *Al-Qisas*, p. 208.
23. See Jassas, op. cit., vol. II, p. 232, *Mughni*, vol. VIII, pp. 320–321.
24. V:48.
25. Shaltut, op. cit., pp. 403–405.
26. Ibid., p. 405; Kasani, *Badai'*, vol. VII, p. 295.
27. *Mishkat al-Masabih*, vol. II, p. 261. This was also reported by the other six collectors of hadith with the exception of Tirmidhi. See Shaltut, op. cit., p. 402.
28. "The information of one" refers to reports narrated by a single companion of the Prophet during his lifetime *('asr as-sahaba)* and by one of the succeeding generation *(attabi'un)*, and so on until it was inscribed in the collections of *ahadith*. On the other hand, there are the reports handed down to the collectors in "regular succession," i.e., reported in each generation by a number of narrators, so that their having collaborated in telling falsehoods is excluded. The first kind of report is known as *hadith ahad* and the second as *hadith mutawatir*, to which the power of establishing a new ruling or law is mostly relegated. See Khallaf, *Usul al-Fiqh*, pp. 36–44; Shaltut, op. cit., pp. 73-76.
29. Shaltut, op. cit., p. 406.

30. Ibid., p. 404; Jassas, op. cit., p. 232; Shafi'i, *Umm*, vol. VI, p. 44, in which both authorities reported the consensus. This does not contradict what was said in chapter II about the legal value of consensus because where it exists its legal value is indisputable. Here it obviously does exist.
31. *Mughni*, pp. 320–321; *Matalib uli al-Nuha*, pp. 63–69; *Umm*, vol. VI, p. 44; *Badai' al-Sanai'*, vol. VII, p. 297 ff.; Hattab's commentary on *Mukhtasar Knalil*, p. 246 ff.
32. *Mudawwanah*, vol. IV, p. 499; Hattab, op. cit., p. 247; *Umm*, p. 52. Prof. J. Schacht in his article, "*Qisas*," in the *Encyclopaedia of Islam* referred to Malik alone as requiring this condition.
33. Shaltut, op. cit., pp. 399–401. It is noteworthy that he rightly describes this latter case as a mere assumption.
34. I have put aside the question of *qisas* for the injuring of a woman by a man at this stage, since it will be referred to later among other disputed points.
35. Ibn Hazm, for example, held that all injuries make the culprit liable to *qisas* (*Muhalla*, vol. X, p. 461). It is interesting that he allows it even for defloration committed by a man; see pp. 455–456.
36. More will be said, about the rights of relatives.
37. *Mishkat al-Masabih*, vol. II, p. 268, where Nasa'i, Darimi and b. Majah are quoted.
38. Ibid., p. 268 where Nasa'i and Darimi are cited. See also Malik, *Al—Muwatta'*, p. 530.
39. Anderson, op. cit., p. 818.
40. Ibn-Nujaym, *Al-Bahr al-Ra'iq Sharh Kanz al-Daqai'q*, vol. VIII, p. 287; Anderson, op.cit.
41. See *Ahkam al-Qur'an*, vol. II, pp. 222–223, and Sarakhsi, *Mabsut*, vol. XXVI, p. 59.
42. *Mughni*, p. 260; *Al-Rawd al-Nadir*, vol. IV, p. 547; *Muhalla*, vol. X, p. 343; Mawwaq's commentary on *Mukhtasar Khalil*, vol. VI, p. 240. It is interesting that some of the Maliki and Hanafi jurists hold a view according to which the varieties of homicide are the first four of the five held by the majority of the Hanafi school. See, for example, Kasani, *Badai'*, p. 233, and Dardir, *Al-Sharh al-Kabir*, a commentary on *Mukhtasar Khalil*, vol. IX, p. 319.
43. Anderson, op. cit., p. 819. However, for generally accepted definitions, see Coulson, *Succession in the Muslim Family*, pp. 177–178.
44. Anderson, op. cit.
45. Coulson, op. cit., p. 177; cf. 'Uda, vol. II, pp. 78–83.
46. For these cases and the different views concerning them, see 'Uda, op. cit., pp. 155–175, and Ahmad Ibrahim, op. cit., pp. 178–194.
47. The *diya* is of two categories: *mughallaza* (in the higher amount) and *mukhaffa* (in the lighter amount). Both consist of one hundred camels; the difference is in kind and age of camels only.
48. Other substitute and incidental punishments are *ta'zir, Kaffara* and *al-hirman min al-mirath wal-wasiya* (deprivation of inheritance and legacy). To the third of these reference has already been made; the first will be discussed later, while the second will not be considered at all because it cannot be classified as a punishment in the legal sense of the word.
49. 'Uda, op.cit., pp. 180–181, 190; among the references he cited, see Dardir, op. cit. vol. IV, p. 237 ff.
50. 'Uda, op. cit., pp. 170-178, and Ibn Hazm, *Muhalla*, p. 388 ff.
51. 'Uda, op. cit., p. 179; Anderson, op. cit., p. 825.
52. Abu Ishaq al-Shirazi, *Muhadhdhab*, vol. II, p. 210.

53. *Mughni,* vol. VIII, p. 375 ff.; *Badai'*, vol. VII, p. 255.
54. *Badai'. op. cit.* The Malikis hold the same view as the Hanafis in relation to accidental homicide; see *Mawwaq,* p. 267.
55. For details see 'Uda, op. cit., pp. 192–198; *"Qisas," "Katl"* and *"Diya"* in the *Encyclopaedia of Islam,* vols. I & II; Anderson, *Homicide in Islamic Law;* and Ibrahim, *Al-Qisas.*
56. Shu'rani, *Mizan,* vol. II, p. 127; *Al-Rawd al-Nadir,* vol. IV, p. 568 ff.
57. *Mughni,* p. 363; Shirbini, *Mughni al-Muhtaj,* vol. IV, p. 45.
58. Shafi'i, *Risalah,* pp. 422–423; *Mughni,* p. 367.
59. *Muwatta',* p. 535.
60. *Mughni;* 'Uda, op. cit., vol. II, p. 261.
61. The first view is held by the Hanbali and Shafi'i schools, while the second is held by the Malikis and, with little modification, the Hanafis. See 'Uda, op.cit. pp. 257-258. It is noteworthy, however, that the same dispute exists in cases of homicide.
62. Jassas, op. cit., vol. I, p. 157 ff.; Baji, *Al-Muntaqa,* vol. VII, p. 103; Nawawi, *Minhaj,* in the margin of *Tuhfat al-Muhtaj,* vol. IV, p. 87; *Mughni,* p. 382; *Muhalla,* vol. XI, p. 50; *Al-Rawd al-Nadir,* p. 559.
63. II:179.
64. *Mughni,* pp. 189–190; *Muhalla,* vol. X, p. 512.
65. *Mughni,* p. 290; Jassas, op. cit., vol. I, p. 145.
66. Shaltut, op. cit., p. 393; *Badai',* vol. VII, p. 238.
67. Ahmad Ibrahim, op. cit., p. 119.
68. A *dhimmi* is a non-Muslim living in a Muslim state.
69. According to the Maliki school, a Muslim is liable to the death penalty for killing a non-Muslim by way of deceit (*ghila*) since it is, in that school's view, a sort of *hiraba* for which the death penalty is prescribed as a *hadd* punishment. See *Mukhtasar Khalil,* with the commentary of al-Mawwaq and al-Hattab, vol. VI, pp. 230–233; Dardir, in the margin of *Hashiyat al-Dusuqi,* vol. IX, p. 383.
70. *Mughni,* vol. VIII, pp. 273–274; *Muhalla,* vol. X, pp. 347–359; *Umm,* vol. VI, pp. 32–34.
71. Jassas, op. cit., pp. 140–144.
72. See above, pp. 116–117.
73. *Muhalla* and Ahmad Ibrahim, op. cit., pp. 121–123.
74. Jassas, vol. I, pp. 142–143.
75. Ahmad Ibrahim, op. cit.; Shaltut, *op. cit.,* pp. 393–395; 'Uda, vol. I, p. 339, and vol. II, p. 124; Sharabasi, *op.cit.,* pp. 132–133.
76. Jassas, op. cit., p. 144.
77. Shalabi, *Al-Fiqh al-Islami,* pp. 200, 204–205.
78. *Badai',* p. 235; Jassas, vol. I, p. 144; Nawawi, *Minhaj,* vol. IV, p. 17; *Mughni,* pp. 285–286.
79. Baji, *Muntaqa,* vol. VII, p. 105; Kinani, *Al-'Iqd al-Munazzam,* vol. II, p. 253.
80. Ahmad Ibrahim, op.cit., pp. 104–108; Shaltut, op. cit. p. 398.
81. See the references cited in n. 81.
82. Ibn Al-'Arabi, *Ahkam al-Qur an,* vol. I, p. 28, and Qurtubi, *Tafsir,* vol. II, p. 249, where it is stated that Tirmidhi denied the authenticity of this *hadith.*
83. Ahmad Ibrahim, op. cit., and Shaltut, op.cit. It is interesting that the same principle is applied to mothers as well; in Arabic the word denoting "father" also means father and grandfather, or, rather generally, all ancestors.
84. See *Al-Rawd al-Nadir,* vol. IV, p. 583–584, where the author quotes the *hadith* stating, "You (the son) and your property belong to your father."

85. Bustani. *Sharh Qanun al-'Uqubat al-Misri,* pp. 14–17.
86. Ibid., pp. 14-17. The same clause was reintroduced in the Egyptian penal-code of 1904, and it remains in the current penal code of 1937.
87. Ibid., pp. 14-17.
88. Abu Haif, *Al-Diya,* p. 134.
89. Ahmad Ibrahim, op. cit., pp. 27–34.
90. Ibid., p. 34.
91. Ahmad Khalifa, *Al-Nazriya al-' Amma lil-Tajrim,* pp. 115–116.
92. Anderson, op. cit., pp. 811–818.
93. Winfield, *On Tort,* 8th Ed., p. 3. This definition is preferred by Clerk and Lindsell in *Torts,* p. 1, and also by Fleming in *The Law of Tort,* 3rd Ed., p. 1.
94. Kenny, *Outlines of Criminal Law,* 16th Ed., p. 539, quoted in Winfield, op. cit., p. 6.
95. Fleming, op. cit., p. 2.
96. It is possible that a criminal court may order a compensatory sum of money to be paid by the wrongdoer to the injured party. But this is distinguished from tort cases in that (1) it is obtainable only in addition to a punishment, or an order in the nature of punishment, inflicted or made by the court, and (2) in a crime, the compensation which may benefit the injured party is not claimable in the first instance, while in a tort it may be. See Winfield, op. cit., p. 6.
97. *Mughni,* p. 307; *Badai',* p. 242 ff.; *Umm,* p. 17; also Hattab's commentary on *Mukhtasar Khalil,* p. 250.
98. Anderson, "Homicide in Islamic Law," op. cit., p. 818.
99. Qurtubi, *Tafsir,* vol. II, pp. 245, 256. See also Shaltut, op. cit., pp. 385–388, where he quotes Razi, Qurtubi, and Muhammad 'Abdu in *Al-Manar (Tafsir).*
100. Shaltut, op. cit.; Ahmad Ibrahim, op. cit., pp. 215–218; 'Uda, op. cit. vol. II, p. 155; Sharabasi, op. cit., p. 134 ff.; Sayed Sabiq, *Fiqh al-Sunna,* vol. X, pp. 61–63.
101. In Shaltut, op. cit., p. 386, attention is drawn to other juristic views, according to which the concept of a punishment for a crime is predominant. See section III above.
102. Qur'an II:178; for the Sunna see Abu Dawud, vol. II, p. 478.
103. Anderson, "Homicide in Islamic Law," op. cit., p. 812.
104. Mawwaq, op. cit., p. 268; Anderson, op. cit. p. 818.
105. See Anderson, op. cit., for other points concerning this topic.
106. Shaltut, op. cit., p. 335–336; Sayed Sabiq, op. cit., p. 23; A. Ibrahim, op. cit., p. 10. However, many points relating to the subject have been omitted from this study since they are beyond its scope, which is limited to the general principles of the theory. of punishment. For details, see the references mentioned throughout this chapter.
107. Exodus, 20:13 and 21:12.
108. XVII:33 and II:178.
109. Exod. 21:23–25.
110. Num. 35:19–21.
111. Matt. 5:38–39. This view was supported by A. Ibrahim, op. cit., p. 5, but opposed by Shaltut, op. cit., p. 326–327, where he quotes Muhammad 'Abdu.
112. Matt. 5:17.
113. See the Qur'anic verses cited previously, together with many others, e.g., XLI:34
114. See the brief account and definition given for the law of homicide in the U.S. in M E. Wolfgang, *Patterns in Criminal Homicide,* pp. 22–24.
115. As far as England is concerned, the argument seems to be about to break out again if it has not already done so. Since the murder of Supt. Gerald Richardson, the

Blackpool Police Chief, on 23 August 1971, many voices have reopened the case, demanding the reintroduction of the death penalty. See *The Times*, 27 August 1971, and the following three issues.

116. From Leo Page, *Crime and the Community*, p. 131. See also Fry, *Arms of the Law*, pp. 181–197.

117. Page, op. cit., p. 132.

118. Even the case of Christie and Evans, which is widely known as an instance of the hanging of an innocent man, is disputed. See Hibbert, *The Roots of Evil*, pp. 417 ff., and pp. 420-421 of the report on the case by Mr. J. Scott Henderson, QC, presented by the Secretary of State for the Home Dept. to Parliament on 14 July 1953 (Cmd. 8896). However, after a second inquiry conducted by Mr. Justice Brabin, The Queen granted Timothy Evans a free pardon on 18 October 1966. For this and the findings of the inquiry see H.C. Hansard, vol. 734, col. 38-40. It is also argued that James Hanratty who was hanged in 1962 was not guilty. See Hibbert, op. cit., pp. 243 and 429; Louis Bloom-Cooper, *The A6 Murderer;* and Paul Foot, *Was Hanratty Guilty?*

119. Page, op. cit., pp. 132–134. The fullest discussion of this topic may be found in *The Royal Commission Report on Capital Punishment, 1949-1953*, pp. 17-24, and Appendix 6, pp. 328–380.

120. *The Royal Commission Report*, op. cit.

121. The Times, 23 April 1970; and Hansard, H.C., volume 830, col. 465.

122. *The Times*, 23 April 1970, and Hansard, H.C., vol. 830, col. 465. Ibrahim, *Al-Qisas*, pp. 236–242; 'Uda, vol. 1, pp. 731–732; Sharabasi, pp. 95–114, where some lawyers' and judges' views as well as those of religious men are cited.

123. 'Uda, pp. 712–714. For corporal punishment in England, cf. Fry, op. cit., p. 108, and appendix F, pp. 234-236.

124. Fry, op. cit., p. 234. See the recommendation of the committee in its report Cmd. 5684, pp. 124–127 (1963 publication). The Advisory Council on the Treatment of Offenders came to largely the same conclusion; see the *Report on Corporal Punishment*, Cmd. 1213, 1960, pp. 26–28.

125. See 'Uda, p. 708 ff., and A. Ibrahim, op. cit., pp. 242–246.

126. 'Uda, vol. I, pp. 668–669.

127. See the references mentioned above on the Law of Tort.

128. Cmds. 1406 and 2323, published by H.M.S.O.

129. Ibid., and 'Uda, vol. I, p. 677 ff. It is apparent that he is speaking here about *diya* as a punishment for quasi-deliberate and accidental homicide, but what he says can be generalized to all cases in which *diya* is due (see especially p. 678). An interesting discussion concerning the difference between compensation and punishment can be found in Qarafi, *Furuq*, vol. I, p. 213, where he is inclined to classify *diya* as a compensation, not a punishment.

130. For details see Hall Williams, *The English Penal System in Transition*, p. 296 ff., and Cmd. 2323. However, the *1971 Criminal Justice Bill* has now become *the Criminal Justice Act, 1972*, and the power of the criminal courts to grant compensation to victims of violent crimes thereby has been enacted.

CHAPTER IV

The Discretionary Punishment (Al-Ta'zir)

As was mentioned previously, the Islamic penal system recognizes three kinds of punishment: *hadd, qisas* and *ta'zir*. In the first chapter we dealt with the *hadd* punishment and in the third with the law of *qisas*, while the second chapter was devoted to discussing two punishments, those for drinking and apostasy, traditionally classified as *hadd*. The punishments for these two crimes were shown to be *ta'zir* and not, as commonly categorized, *hadd* punishments. In this chapter the third kind of punishment recognized in Islamic penal system will be discussed.

I. Definition

Etymologically the word *ta'zir* is derived from the verb *azar*, which means to prevent, to respect, and to reform.[1] The verb has been used in its first and second meanings in the Qur'an.[2] However, in Islamic legal writing *ta'zir* denotes a punishment aimed first at preventing the criminal from committing further crimes and secondly at reforming him. The dual meaning is likely to recall the confusion between the reformative and deterrent theories of punishment. In the Islamic penal system, *ta'zir* is a typical case of this confusion. In his well-known book, *Tabsirat al-Hukkam*, Ibn Farhun tried to define the aim of *ta'zir* by saying that it is a "disciplinary, reformative, and deterrent punishment."[3] This definition suggests that the two aspects, reformation and deterrence, are combined here. Since "disciplinary" can mean nothing but individual deterrence, it is correct to say that it is the real basis of *ta'zir*, while reformation becomes, in fact, a means of deterring.

However, *ta'zir* was defined as "discretionary punishment to be delivered for transgression against God, or against an individual for which

96

there is neither fixed punishment nor penance *(kaffara).''*[4] This definition automatically excludes all crimes for which *qisas* is prescribed, for where *hadd, kaffara,* or *qisas* are applied, *ta'zir* cannot intervene nor replace any of them. It is possible that *ta'zir* may appear as an alternative and/or additional punishment in some cases, as will be seen shortly, but not as the sole punishment.[5]

According to some orientalists, *ta'zir* punishment is not mentioned in the Qur'an and the Sunna has very little to report concerning it.[6] This view leads us to investigate the possible origin *(asl)* of the *ta'zir* punishment in both the Qur'an and Sunna. From this starting point, we will discuss the different aspects of the punishment, with special reference to *ta'zir* by means of the death penalty and by seizure of property, as well as to the possibility of inflicting *ta'zir* in addition to other punishments, e.g., *hadd* or *qisas.*

II. *Ta'zir* in the Qur'an and Sunna

It must be admitted that the word *ta'zir* was never used in the Qur'an or in the Sunna in the sense in which it is used in Islamic legal writing. At the same time, both the Qur'an and the Sunna referred to some types of crimes for which there is no fixed punishment and concerning which it was left to the judge or the ruler to decide what sort of punishment to impose and the manner of inflicting it. One instance of such crimes is mentioned in the Qur'an. "As for the two of you (males) who are guilty of it, punish them both . . .[7]" This verse, according to the commentators, refers to homosexual relations between men.[8] The order "punish them both" is given to the ruler of the community without specifying the sort of punishment, its amount, or how it must be carried out. The decision, therefore, is entirely left to the ruler or the judge.

Another case in which the authority to punish is given in the Qur'an in similarly flexible terms, as in the above case, is stated in the following verse: "As for those (women) from whom you fear disloyalty and ill-conduct, admonish them (first), (next) refuse to share their beds, and (last) beat them (lightly)."[9] This verse is concerned with the treatment of wives who rebel against their husbands. Although the methods of dealing with such wives are stated, and are to be used consecutively, a good deal is left to the discretion of the husband, who is the head of the household. He is given a certain amount of freedom in deciding how to use his authority.[10]

It was this authority which jurists considered as the origin of the *ta'zir* punishment *(al-asl fi-l ta'zir)*.[11] This view may be interpreted by way of analogy *(qiyas)*. If it is true that the husband, as the ruler of the basic unit of society, the family, has been given such an authority in order to safeguard the interest of his unit and its members, then the ruler of the whole society and his representatives, e.g., the judges, must have the same authority over the society or the parts of it with which they are concerned. In this way rulers, and likewise judges, are enabled to safeguard the society's interest when it is threatened by actions or omissions which fall outside the very limited area of the fixed punishments *(al-hudud)* and the punishment of retaliation *(al-qisas)*. hudud) and the punishment of retaliation *(al-qisas)*.

A third verse in the Qur'an may be even more directly concerned with *ta'zir*. In the first part of this verse a general principle is enunciated: "The recompense of an evil is a like evil . . ."[12] This establishes a legal rule dealing with the treatment of any misdeed, namely, that it cannot be punished with anything but a penalty commensurate with the misdeed. This "equality" does not indicate the minimum penalty but the maximum one, for the later part of the verse states: "But if a person forgives and makes reconciliation, his reward is due from God. . ."[13] As far as I know, this verse, "The recompense of an evil. . .," has not been cited in this context. However, I see it as a valid origin for the law of *ta'zir* because it is assumed that the person who is liable to *ta'zir* has done what is considered evil either to the community or to another individual. His punishment, therefore, may be justified by the rule laid down in this verse. At the same time, the other two verses in Surah IV may be understood as applications of this principle.

Accordingly, it cannot rightly be said that the "Qur'an does not know this kind of punishment." On the contrary, the Qur'an laid down the principle from which the *ta'zir* punishment was deduced and also mentioned some of its applications. It was the jurists' reluctance to admit the Qur'anic origin of this punishment which led to such a dubious statement. By giving more attention to these three verses, one may be able to realize that the legal principles of *ta'zir* are expressed in the Qur'an by implication, if not directly.

More examples and cases of *ta'zir* may be found in the Sunna. All these cases were used afterwards, in one way or another, to construct the juristic formulation of the *ta'zir* as part of the Islamic penal system. As far as the jurists are concerned, they are indebted to these Prophetic reports for their knowledge and understanding of *ta'zir*. It is true that the decisions of the Prophet's companions relating to *ta'zir* appear more clearly in the manuals of Islamic law, especially the decisions of 'Omar, but these decisions are in turn based on the sayings and practices of the Prophet himself.[14] Indeed, many examples of Prophetic reports concerned with *ta'zir* are known. The following are some of them, taken from both the words and actions of the Prophet.

The most important example of Prophetic practice concerning the *ta'zir* punishment is the punishment for drinking. As the view that this is a *ta'zir* punishment was fully explained in Chapter II, we do not need to dwell on it here. And this is by no means the only example. Once a companion of the Prophet injured a slave of his as a punishment for having had sexual relations with a female slave. When the Prophet saw the injured slave, he freed him. This was a punishment to the slave's owner because of the injury he had inflicted on him.[15] Muslim and Abu-Dawud also transmit a *hadith* according to which the Prophet deprived a man of his share of the spoils of a battle because of a misdeed he committed against the commander of the army.[16]

Among the Muslims of Madina who did not go with the Prophet to the battle of Tabuk were Ka'b b. Malik, Murarah b. al-Rabi', and Hilal b. Umaya. After the Prophet's return to Madina, some of those who had not gone with him gave him false excuses, but these three men told the truth: that they had had no real reason for staying at home in Madina and not joining the campaign. The Prophet ordered all Muslims to avoid any contact with them; their wives were not even allowed to share their beds. Fifty days later, a Qur'anic verse was revealed stating that Allah had forgiven the three and accepted their repentance.[17] This Prophetic order to avoid and ignore the men was a *ta'zir* punishment imposed upon them for their failure to respond to the call to arms.[18]

To turn to the Prophet's words concerning the *ta'zir* punishment, we must again refer to Chapter II, where the punishment for apostasy was mentioned. There it was explained that the penalty for apostasy can be nothing but a sort of *ta'zir*. Again, this is not the only *hadith* concerning the subject. For stealing fruit of a value less than that for which the *hadd* punishment is to be applied, the Prophet adjudged that the thief must pay "double its value and be liable to punishment." The "doubled value" is a fine which can be interpreted as a *ta'zir*. But a more obvious reference to *ta'zir* is the last clause of the *hadith*, "and be liable to punishment," because both the kind and amount of punishment here are left entirely to the discretion of the judge.[19] Again in relation to the payment of *zakat*, the

Prophet said, "Whoever gives it will be rewarded (by God), and whoever refuses to give it, it will be taken from him; and we will take one-half of his property, not for Muhammad or his family but for the state treasury." This fining of the offender is also a sort of *ta'zir* punishment.[20]

The Qur'an enjoins that if a debtor is in financial distress, the creditor is to give him more time to pay his debt, yet when a rich man refused to pay his debt, the Prophet allowed him to be punished. In the *hadith* reporting this incident the Prophet did not explain what kind of punishment he meant to be inflicted for this behavior, or how much.[21] This is so, I think, because such a situation must be dealt with in the light of the circumstances of both the creditor and the debtor, as well as the general financial condition of the community at a given time. What is important, however, is that this *hadith* does exemplify a case in which the Prophet ordered a *ta'zir* punishment.[22]

In the light of these examples, we reach the conclusion that *ta'zir* punishment is based on the previously-mentioned Qur'anic verses and prophetic reports. It is true that the development of this system of punishment was expressed at a comparatively later stage by the different schools of law, but this does not justify the claim that the Qur'an does not contain references to it and that the Sunna has very little to record concerning it.[23]

It has been important to clarify the Qur'anic and Prophetic origins of this punishment for two reasons. The first is that these have not been examined, and the second is that such an examination will help to establish our viewpoint concerning many of the ensuing topics.

III. Kinds of *Ta'zir* Punishments

Unlike hadd punishment for *qisas*, *ta'zir* punishments are not determined in specific terms. The judge, in cases of crimes for which *ta'zir* punishment is prescribed, has a wide variety of punishments from which he can choose the one suitable to the particular crime, according to the criminal's circumstances, his record, and his psychological condition.[24] The judge's authority is limited by his obligation not to order a punishment which is not allowed by Islamic law; he cannot, for examplle, order the offender to be whipped naked.[25]

Here the punishments allowed as *ta'zir* will be discussed briefly and the most important of them will be dealt with in more detail. However, these punishments are by no means the only punishments which can be

rescribed in cases of *ta'zir*. That is to say, any punishment which may serve
ie purpose of *ta'zir*, namely, to prevent any further crime and reform the
ffender, can be used as long as it does not contradict the general princi-
les of Islamic law. The ensuing punishments represent what was known,
nd actually used, in Islamic legal texts and practice, but any other useful
unishment may also be legally used.[26]
Apart from the determination of the punishment, the ruler or judge is
raditionally assigned the right to determine whether an act is criminal or
ot. This is the key concept of *ta'zir*, which is defined as a punishment
or "any transgression." Transgressions cannot be foreseen; hence this
ight has been granted to the ruler or judge to meet the needs of the socie-
y and protect it against every kind of transgression.[27]

II. 1. Admonition *(al-Wa'z)*

Admonition means reminding the person who has committed a trans-
ression that he has done an unlawful thing. It was prescribed in the
Qur'an IV: 34 as the first stage in dealing with disobedient wives. The
urpose of admonition is to remind the offender if he has forgotten, or to
nform him if he was unaware, that he has done something wrong.[28] This
ort of treatment is to be restricted to those who commit minor offences
or the first time, provided the judge thinks it is enough to reform the
ffender and restrain him from any further transgression.[29]

II. 2. Reprimand *(al-Tawbikh)*

Reprimand may be through any word or act which the judge feels to
e sufficient to serve the purpose of *ta'zir*. The jurists usually refer to
ome specific words and acts as a means of reprimand, but it is not neces-
ary to concentrate on these means as they vary according to the offence
nd the offender. Such a reprimand led a Companion of the Prophet, as an
ct of penitence for having insulted someone, to set free his slaves.[30]

II. 3. Threat *(al-Tahdid)*

Threat is a *ta'zir* penalty by means of which the offender may be in-
luced to mend his behavior out of fear of punishment. It may consist of

threatening him with punishment if he repeats what he has done, or by
pronouncing a sentence against him, the execution of which is delayed
until he commits another offence (within a given period of time). Apart
from the normal condition of the suitability of the *ta'zir* punishment, im
plementation of the threat, in the event of another offence, must clearly be
intended.[31]

This way of dealing with offenders who commit offences punishable
by *ta'zir* may be compared with the modern penal concept of suspended
sentences which is known to almost all modern penal systems. Under the
English Criminal Justice Act of 1967 (Section 39), for example, a cour
which passes a sentence of imprisonment for a term of not more than two
years may suspend the sentence for a specified period. This period i
known as the "operational period" of the suspended sentence; it may no
be less than one year nor more than three years. Under the Islamic pena
system the matter of determining the "operational period" is left entirely
to the judge's discretion. Another difference between the two systems i
that under English law a court has no power to suspend a sentence othe
than imprisonment, whereas traditional Islamic law grants the judge the
authority to suspend any sentence, whether of imprisonment of or anything
else.[32]

III. 4. Boycott *(al-Hajr)*

Boycott as a *ta'zir* punishment is recommended by the Qur'an (IV
34), and it was practiced by the Prophet in the case of the men who did
not participate in the campaign of Tabuk.[33] It was also imposed by 'Omar upon a
man who used to ask about and discuss difficult words in the Qur'an in order to
confuse people.[34] According to some writers, boycott as a punishment is no
practical in our time because it was based on a powerful religious feeling among
people which no longer exists. The defendants of this punishment may argue
that it can be inflicted by preventing the offender from communicating with
other people, but it would then become a sort of imprisonment rather than the
intended boycott.[35]

III. 5. Public Disclosure *(al-Tashhir)*

Public disclosure has been known as a punishment since the earlies slamic times. The Prophet sent a man to collect alms *(zakat)*; when he returned to Madina he gave some of what he had collected to the Prophet but kept the rest, claiming it had been given to him as a gift. The Prophet then addressed the people, saying, "I appointed one of you to do some public services; afterwards he divided what he had collected into two portions: one for the public treasury and the other for himself. If the appointed man had stayed in his father's or his mother's home, would anyone have given him a gift or not?"[36]

According to Shurahyh, a well-known judge who served under 'Omar and 'Ali, the false witness must be publicly identified in order to warn people not to trust him;[37] on this point all the schools of Islamic law are agreed.[38] The means of public disclosure usually consisted of the taking of the offender by some of the judge's representatives to every part of the city and telling the people that he had committed an offence for which he had received a *ta'zir* punishment. The purpose of this punishment was to call the public's attention to the fact that this offender was not to be trusted.[39]

Public disclosure is not made in the same manner in our time. As the media of public information have developed enormously, it may be done by publishing the court judgment in the newspapers, by broadcasting it on the radio and television, or by any other means which will inform people concerning the offence.

According to the jurists, this punishment is relevant for offences in which the trustworthiness of the offender is questionable; however, it may also be used for any other offense for which the judge considers it suitable. Finally, it must be noted that it is an additional punishment. The jurists usually prescribe other punishments such as imprisonment or beating for offences in which they also advise public disclosure.[40]

III. 6. Fines and the Seizure of Property *(al-Gharamah wal-Musadarah)*

It was mentioned previously that the Prophet imposed financial penalties as *ta'zir* punishments. But the jurists are divided into three groups concerning the legality of this. According to some, it is illegal to punish by fine or by seizure of property; the second group regards it as legal, while the third group regards it as legal only if the offender does not repent.

The first view is held by the Hanafi school and some of the Shafi'is.[41]

According to Malik, Ahmad b. Hanbal, Abu Yusuf (the famous Hanafi jurist), nd some of the Shafi'is, financial punishments are allowed as *ta'zir*[42] The Hanafi commentators explained that the view of Abu Yusu means that the judge or ruler does not take the offender's money for th public treasury but in order to keep it away from him until he has re pented. They support this view by saying that no one is allowed to tak another's money without legal reason *(bisabab shar'i)*. If it later appear that the offender will not repent, then the ruler may order the money to b spent on public requirements.[43] The reason they give for this explanatio is that allowing the judge or the ruler to take the offender's money for th public treasury might subject such a practice to abuse by unjust judges o rulers.[44]

On the other hand, the jurists who deny financial punishment as lawful *ta'zir* punishment claim that it was legalized in the beginning o Islam but abrogated afterwards. The first jurist who expressed this view was the Hanafi jurist Tahawi in his famous book, *Sharh Ma'ani al-Athar (Explanation of the Meanings of the Traditions)*.[45] This claim of abroga tion was, however, strongly rejected by Ibn Taymiyya and his studen Ibn al-Qayyim, on evidence taken mainly from the Prophet's practices an from some of his Companions' decisions.[46] Ibn al-Qayyim added,

These are well-known cases which have been accurately reported. Those who claim that financial punishment was abrogated are wrong. Their view may be refuted by the cases ascribed to great Companions of the Prophet. Neither the Qur'an nor the Sunna can help them in supporting their claim, nor is there any consensus about it. Even if there were a consensus, it would have no power to abrogate the Sunna. The only thing they may say is: in our school's view it is not allowed. This means that they take their own view as a standard of what is accepted and what is not.[47]

Other Hanbali, Hanafi, and Maliki commentators also hold this view and defend it mainly in Ibn al-Qayyim's words. According to Ibn a Qayyim's evidence, both elements of the financial punishment (i.e., fin and seizure of property) are allowed in Islamic law. In some cases th amount is determined by the Prophet's practice, e.g., in cases of theft i which the value involved does not reach the minimum value required fo inflicting the *hadd* punishment, refusing payment of *zakat*, etc., but i other cases it is not so determined, and it is left to the judge to decide ho much the culprit should be fined. Indeed, there is nothing to stop th lawmaker of any Muslim country from listing crimes and their fines as h requires them to be applied by the courts.

The statement that "there are no fines in Islamic law" is therefor patently incorrect.[49] The most that can be claimed is that fines, or rather financial punishments, are a subject of controversy, but it cannot be justifiably said that the Islamic penal system does not recognize this sort of punishment.

III. 7. Imprisonment *(al-Habs)*

In Islamic law imprisonment is of two kinds, either that for a definite term or that for an indefinite term. Imprisonment for a definite term can be imposed for minor offenses, since the jurists prefer flogging as the punishment for major or dangerous *ta'zir* offenses.[50] The minimum period for imprisonment is one day.[51] But the schools hold different views concerning the maximum period.

The Maliki, Hanafi, and Hanbali schools do not fix a maximum period for the *ta'zir* imprisonment, because it varies for each offense and from one individual to another.[52] According to the Shafi'i school, the maximum period of imprisonment is one month for investigation and six months for punishment, and, in any case, it must last for less than a year. This view is based on an analogy *(qiyas)* with the punishment for *zina* committed by an unmarried person (fornication). Banishment in this case is for one year, and consequently imprisonment as a *ta'zir* punishment must not last longer than the banishment allowed for fornication, which is a *hadd* punishment according to the Shafi'i jurists.[53] However, among the Shafi'i jurists one can also find another view which is similar to that of the three other schools.[54] Accordingly, it may be said that the majority view is that the judge is free to determine the maximum period for a definite term of imprisonment as he sees fit, depending on the criminal and his crime. According to all the schools of Islamic law, it is also allowed to impose imprisonment as an additional punishment if circumstances so require.[55]

As for imprisonment for an unlimited term, it is imposed on habitual criminals who, in the judge's view, cannot be reformed by ordinary punishments. All the schools of Islamic law authorize this punishment to last either until the criminal's repentance or, until his death in the case of a dangerous criminal.[56] This sort of imprisonment is similar to that of the *hadd* punishment for armed robbery *(hiraba)*, for which one of the punishments prescribed is banishment, interpreted as imprisonment, to be enforced until the achievement of the criminal's repentance or until his death. However, there is an important condition for the imposition of this punishment as *ta'zir*, namely, that it can only be applied as long as the reform of the offender by any other punishment is impossible.[57] It is on this condition only that unlimited imprisonment is justified.

Another *ta'zir* punishment, with which modern writers on the subject have dealt separately, is banishment *(al-nafy)*. *Nafi* was referred to when we dealt with the punishment for fornication. It may be recalled that the Hanafi school considers this punishment as an additional *ta'zir* punishment for fornication, while other schools consider it as *hadd*, regarding the *hadd* punishment for fornication as two-fold, i.e., one hundred lashes and one year's banishment.[58] Apart from the crime of fornication, banishment is considered as a *ta'zir* punishment for offenders who may encourage other people to imitate their deviant behavior.[59]

Banishment may last either for the period mentioned in the sentence or until the offender's behavior is believed to have improved.[60] However, banishment nowadays cannot consist of anything but imprisonment. Banishment may be from one place, e.g., from one city, to another in the same country, or from the criminal's country of origin (or residence) to a foreign country. However, the former does not really serve the purpose of banishment, which is to prevent the offender from encouraging others to imitate him. The latter is not possible today, because no country will accept offenders from other countries as immigrants; although it was a common practice in many European countries during colonial times to banish offenders to a colony, this can no longer be done. Under present-day conditions, therefore, the only possible form banishment can take is imprisonment.

III. 8. Flogging *(al-Jald)*

Flogging is a common punishment in Islamic penal law. It has already been referred to as a *hadd* punishment for the crime of *qadhf* (80 lashes), and for *zina* committed by an unmarried person (100 lashes). As a *ta'zir* punishment, it was mentioned when we dealt with the crime of drinking. The point which will be discussed here is the maximum number of lashes allowed in *ta'zir* cases. To Muslim jurists this problem is known as the possibility of exceeding the *hadd* punishment in cases of *ta'zir* (*hal yutajawaz bil-ta'zir miqdar al-hadd*).

The most liberal view in this context is the Maliki one, according to which the *ta'zir* punishment may exceed the *hadd* punishment as long as the judge or the ruler thinks the circumstances require it.[61] The opposite view is held by the Zahiri and Zaydi schools and a section of the Hanbali school, who hold that flogging as a *ta'zir* punishment cannot exceed 10 lashes.[62] Intermediate views are held by the Hanafi and Shafi'i' schools and some Hanbali scholars. There is no unamimity about the maximum number of lashes among the holders of these views; according to some it is 75 lashes, others hold it to be 99, and some fix it at 39, while others do not allow more than 20.[63]

This controversy is based on two prophetic reports. The first, in which the Prophet forbade more than 10 lashes to be inflicted except in cases of *hadd* punishment, was reported by Muslim and Bukhari.[64] The second was reported by Bayhaqi. In this *hadith* the Prophet referred to those who exceed the limits of the *hadd* punishment in a non-*hadd* crime as transgressors *(mu'tadun)*.[65]

The prevalent view concerning the first *hadith* is that it was abrogated; this is deduced from the fact that the Companions of the Prophet did not act in accordance with it. It is related that 'Omar and 'Ali inflicted more than 10 lashes in cases of *ta'zir* with no objection from the other Companions; hence the *hadith*, according to the majority view, must have been abrogated.[66]

Another interpretation of this *hadith* was given by Ibn Taymiyya and Ibn al-Qayyim. They saw this *hadith* as relevant to the relations between father and son, husband and wife, and master and servant, i.e., relationships in which one may need to use some means of punishment for disciplinary reasons. In such cases, if the appropriate means is beating, it must not exceed 10 lashes. But this report has nothing to do with the relationship between the individual and the state, and the amount of *ta'zir* punishment, if it happens to be by flogging, is left to the authority concerned.[67] According to this view there is no need for the claim of abrogation since the *hadith* is not relevant to the case in question. However, the jurists who do not accept either the obrogation theory or the interpretation of Ibn Taymiyya and his companion hold the view that a *ta'zir* punishment by flogging should not exceed 10 lashes.[68]

The second *hadith*, although incompletely transmitted *(mursal)*,[69] was accepted by all the Sunni schools except the Maliki. Those who accepted this *hadith* interpreted it in different ways; consequently, they hold varying views about the maximum *ta'zir* punishment. The first interpretation is that this *hadith* forbade the *ta'zir* punishment to exceed the lesser *hadd* punishment. However, jurists differ as to what the lesser *hadd* punishment is: some consider it to be 80 lashes (the *hadd* punishment for slander or *qadhf*), while others consider it to be the *hadd* punishment for a slave, which is 40 lashes (i.e., half of the freeman's *hadd* punishment). The second interpretation is that the *hadith* prohibited the *ta'zir's* equalling the *hadd* punishment in cases of incomplete crimes for which, if they were completed, a *hadd* punishment would be prescribed. That is to say, a crime of theft for which the *hadd* cannot be inflicted may result in a *ta'zir* of 100 lashes, since the original punishment is the amputation of the offender's hand. A sexual relationship which has not involved intercourse may be punished by more than 100 lashes if the culprit is a *muhsan* or married; but it should not reach 100 lashes if he or she is unmarried because the original *hadd* punishment is 100 lashes. Other interpretations are also available, but they are less important than these two.[70]

The minimum number of lashes allowed as *ta'zir* was also discussed. Some jurists fixed it at 3, but the majority does not agree with this view because it contradicts the main feature of *ta'zir*, i.e., its variation from one crime to another according to the offender's character and other circumstances.[71]

However, the view expressed by Ibn Taymiyya and his student, Ibn al-Qayyim, seems the most relevant both practically and logically. In practice they allow any suitable punishment and avoid the strict limitation imposed on the ruler's power to inflict *ta'zir* punishment. From the logical point of view, they limit the *hadith* concerning the number of lashes allowed for non-*hadd* punishments to a particular province and are consequently not compelled to use the abrogation claim as other scholars do. This, too, is in harmony with a principle of Islamic law which recommends the application of legal verdicts rather than their neglect (*i'mal al-kalam khayrun min ihmalihi*).[72]

III. 9. The Death Penalty *(al-Ta'zir bil-Qatl)*

Ta'zir punishment is that part of the Islamic penal system which deals with the less serious offences. The death penalty is usually imposed for the most serious crimes; in Islamic law, as we have seen, it is the punishment for two *hadd* offences and, in the form of *qisas*, for homicide. The jurists, accordingly, are normally against its being inflicted as a *ta'zir* punishment,[73] but exceptional cases in which *ta'zir* by the death penalty is allowed are mentioned in the texts of almost every school.

Examples of offenders who can be awarded the death penalty are given in the Hanafi texts: the habitual homosexual, the murderer on whom *qisas* cannot be imposed because of the means used in the crime (*al-qatl bil-muthqil*), and the habitual thief who attacks a man's house and who is not to be prevented from doing harm by means of other punishments.[74] For the Maliki School, "the principle that the *ta'zir* punishment should fit the crime, the criminal, and the victim is of absolute application. Thus, the death penalty is permissible in certain cases, where either the offence itself is of a very serious nature, such as spying for the enemy, or propagating heretical doctrines, or practices which split the community, or the criminal is a habitual offender whose wickedness can only be so stopped."[75] The Shafi'i and Hanbali schools allow the death penalty to be imposed in the same cases for which it is allowed by the Malikis.[76]

However, it must be remembered that there are some Prophetic reports which allow the death penalty as a *ta'zir* punishment; accordingly the various relevant views must be justified in its light. Some of these *ahadith* have been mentioned before. Here reference can be made to the cases of spying for the enemy in which the Prophet ordered the offender to be sentenced to death.[77]

At the same time, the death penalty as a *ta'zir* punishment is an exception; it is therefore to be applied in the minimum possible number of cases, i.e., only when made necessary either by the criminal's character or by the nature of the offence. Accordingly, one should support the view expressed by some contemporary writers that the ruler or legislator in each country must restrict its application only to cases in which it is necessary for the above reasons. Such a severe penalty should not be left to the discretion of the judge, but applied only according to legislation enacted by the authority concerned.[78] While it may be said that there is no harm in leaving the death penalty to the judge's discretion, since the jurists have defined the cases in which it may be inflicted, this makes no difference because the jurists' decisions are only taken, and can only be taken, as simple illustrations and guides.[79]

III. 10. *Ta'zir* as an Additional Punishment

Islamic law, generally speaking, imposes one punishment for one crime. This principle is taken from the Qur'an, where a related rule is expressed in many chapters.[80] But exceptions to this principle were permitted by the jurists with regard to some crimes. The Hanafi school allows *ta'zir* punishment to be imposed in addition to any *hadd* punishment when the circumstances justify it. It is on this basic principle that they interpret the punishment of one year's banishment for the fornicator, as has been mentioned before. Ibn Taymiyya declared that the Hanafi school permits the *hadd* punishment to be exceded if the authority concerned, i.e.,the *imam*, thinks it necessary in certain cases.[81] This school allows even the death penalty to be inflicted for repeated crimes, any one of which does not deserve this punishment, terming it *al-qatl siyasatan,* i.e., the death penalty justified on the basis of the public interest.[82] The punishment which may be added to the *hadd* can be nothing but a *ta'zir* punishment.

According to the Malikis, *ta'zir* punishment may be inflicted in cases of wounds or injury, even when *qisas* is applicable and has actually been inflicted. They consider this punishment to be an effective deterrent for the criminal himself, as well as for other potential criminals.[83]

From these examples, it is clear that *ta'zir* may be either the original punishment for crimes which have no fixed punishment or an additional punishment for crimes which deserve *hadd* or *qisas* punishment. It is worth mentioning that under the doctrine of *ta'zir,* the Islamic penal system allows the judge to pass more severe sentences against a recidivist offender. The above-mentioned examples are usually quoted as evidence for this situation.[84]

To summarize what has been said in this section, *ta'zir* punishments range from a simple reprimand to imprisonment, and from flogging to the death penalty. Fines and seizure of property may also be imposed. There is no restriction, as far as the Islamic law manuals are concerned, on the judge's authority to choose the punishment he considers suitable for the crime, the criminal's character, and the victim, where applicable. It has been suggested that *ta'zir* punishments must be listed in accordance with the various crimes for which they may be imposed, and particularly that restriction must be put on the cases in which capital punishment is applicable. *Ta'zir* is not always applied as the only punishment, but it may also be applied in addition to other punishments if necessary.

IV. The Judge's Discretionary Power

The most common notion about *ta'zir* is that the ruler or the judge, is completely free in the determination of the offences and their sanctions. The extensive scope of the ruler's or judge's discretion outside the field of *hadd* and *qisas* offenses is indeed intolerable to modern legal thinking and is contrary to the accepted constitutional principles of today. It was described by a contemporary *Shari'a* scholar as "extensive powers at the ruler's disposal, to discipline anyone, for anything, with any punishment *(yu addibu man sha' 'ala ma sha' bi ma sha')*."[85] Such a wide scope of discretionary power is entirely contrary to the universally-accepted constitutional principle of *"nulla poena sine lege."* This section will be devoted to illustrating that the discretionary power of judges is, in fact, much more limited than is sometimes imagined.

It is important that jurists have shown some evidence of a desire to make *ta'zir* offences and their sanctions more specific. But this will not be dealt with here as it can only be understood as "simple illustrations and guides."[86] However, the judge must do his best, by means of conscientious reasoning *(ijtihad)*, to choose the proper punishment in each case of *ta'zir*.[87] Thus, he "must not pronounce penalties at his mere whim or pleasure, or turn from one to another in an arbitrary fashion, for this would be injustice *(fusuq)* and contrary to consensus *(ijma')*."[88] Therefore, the judge's discretionary power in relation to the punishment must be interpreted as his obligation to pronounce the most suitable penalty to fit the case in question, in order to correct the offender's behavior and safeguard the public interest by preventing futher offences.

The ruler's (or judge's) authority in the determination of *ta'zir* offences is our main concern in this section. *Ta'zir* offences may be either of the same essential nature as the *hadd* offences but of a less serious degree or may qualify simply as "transgressions."[89] In both cases, the determination of the punishment is at the discretion of the judge in the above-mentioned mannner. But in the case of a "transgression," it is usually said that the ruler or judge is required to determine the offence as well. To establish how much truth this idea contains we must refer to the definition of *ta'zir* as a punishment for transgression against God or against an individual for which there is neither *hadd* punishment nor *kaffara*.

The right to determine what is a transgression and what is not is reserved in Islam for God alone, as Muslims hold that the *Shari'a* is the final statement of God's law for mankind.[90] God's Will is expressed in the Qur'an and the accurately related Prophetic reports, al-ahadith al-sahihah, which are known as the Sunna. The Qur'an and the Sunna contain many statements which prohibit various types of human activity and classify them as sins (*m'asi*). In relation to these forbidden acts the ruler's or judge's task is to choose the punishment applicable in each case, but he has nothing to do with the determination of the offense as it has already been determined by the Qur'an or the Sunna. Examples of such cases are innumerable, but it will help to give some of the most important ones.

IV. 1. Usury *(al-Riba)*

The Qur'an prohibits dealing in usury in five verses contained in Surahs II, III and LIX. One of the verses states, "O believers, fear God, and give up the usury that is outstanding if you are believers. But if you do not, then take notice that God shall wage war against you. . ." (II: 279). Another verse says: "God has permitted trade and forbidden usury (II:275)." Usury is therefore a prohibited activity; one who engages in it deserves punishment which has not been fixed in the Qur'an or Sunna. Here the duty of the judge is to choose the proper punishment for this prohibited behavior, but he does not determine the crime.

The jurists are not unanimous about what may be considered usury and what may not; hence, the ruler, or the judge, must decide this question. Accordingly, some may argue that this is not the determination of the offence but simply the determination of whether or not the offender's act constitutes prohibited conduct. This, in fact, is the role of any court in relation to any sort of crime: to establish, in the light of the evidence provided, the offender's guilt, after which the penalty can be pronounced.

IV. 2. False Testimony *(Shahadat al-Zur)*

False testimony is condemned in the Qur'an and Muslims are commanded to bear witness to the truth. One verse enjoins: "O believers, be securers of justice, witnesses for God, even though it be against yourselves, or your parents and kinsmen." Another verse describes believers as "those who witness no falsehood." A third verse orders the believers to "shun the abomination of idols, and shun the speaking of falsehoods."[91] The jurists have said a good deal concerning the punishment of a false witness, but the crime itself is defined by the Qur'an and what the jurists have said applies to the stage of choosing the punishment for the crime rather than determining the nature of the crime itself.

IV. 3. Breach of Trust *(Khiyanat al-Amanah)*

The Qur'an states, "God commands you to deliver trusts back to their owners." Another verse reads, "O believers, betray not God and the Messenger, and betray not your trusts."[92] There are many other Qur'anic verses concerned with breaches of trust, but these two are sufficient to indicate that these offences were formulated in the Qur'an.

IV. 4. Insults *(al-Sabb)*

The Qur'an forbids Muslims to insult other human beings, including those who are not of the same faith. As for the Muslims' interaction with each other, the Qur'an commands, "O believers, let not any people scoff at another people who may be better than they; neither let women scoff at women who may be better than themselves. And find not fault with one another, neither revile one another by nicknames. An evil name is ungodliness after belief."[93] According to these verses and other similar ones, the jurists classified insults as a *ta'zir* offence.

IV. 5. Bribery *(al-Rishwa)*

Just as the Qur'an forbade usury and considered it an unlawful way of making money, all other dishonest means of making money are likewise prohibited. Concerning bribery the Qur'an says, "Consume not your property among yourselves in vanity, neither proffer it to the judge, that you may sinfully consume a portion of other men's property intentionally."[94] Based on the prohibition of bribery established by this verse, it is considered a *ta'zir* offense for which the authority concerned (the ruler or the judge) may impose a punishment.

Many *ahadith* are reported for all the above examples, sometimes to explain what was meant by a Qur'anic verse and sometimes to illustrate how hated and wrong the forbidden behavior is in the sight of God and his Messenger.[95] These five examples are enough to prove that *ta'zir* offences are mainly established by the Qur'an. This should not be taken to mean that the ruler has no right, outside the province of the Qur'an or the Sunna, to establish offences and their punishments, but that the right to do so is limited to what is necessary for the achievement of the aims and goals approved by Islamic law.

V. The Determination of Offences Under the Principle of *Ta'zir*

The final end of Islamic law, the Shari'a, is the protection of religion, life, lineage, mind, and property. This is agreed upon by all Muslim jurists, although it has not been mentioned in the Qur'an or the Sunna in these exact words. This agreement is achieved by way of deduction from all the judgments in the Islamic legal sources.[96] All the obligations and prohibitions of the Islamic Shari'a were ordained for the achievement of these ends. The ruler must therefore act in the public interest to protect these five basic aspects of human life. Any transgression against one or more of them should be considered unlawful and, if necessary, punishable.

Some of the possible transgressions have been mentioned in terms of prohibition, *tahrim* in the Qur'an and the Sunna, but there are many others which have not been mentioned there. The ruler's power to consider or establish these transgressions as offences and to determine their sanctions may be considered here. Some Muslim jurists refer to this power when they add to the above five basic aspects the goal of eliminating any transgression.[97] The ruler's power must be exercised on the basis of the general principles of the law and with the intention of protecting the aim of these principles which relate to the public interest. Moreover, the ruler's power to determine such offences and their punishments is not based only on juristic reasoning (*ijtihad*) but also on the general commands which prohibit transgression and corruption.

These commands are expressed in several Qur'anic verses[98] and *ahidith*. Several of these Qur'anic verses command the Muslim community to "enjoin what is right and forbid what is wrong." The right and the wrong are not listed in one place in the Qur'an or the Sunna, but they can be known by investigation of the whole text of the Qur'an and the collection of *ahadith*. Even then, they cannot be known in terms of details but rather in general terms, according to which each individual act can be classified.[99] In this province, the ruler can exercise his legislative power to enforce the "right" and prohibit the "wrong," even when what he enforces or prohibits is not mentioned specifically in either the Qur'an or the Sunna.

This legislative power of the ruler may be felt to contradict what was said above concerning the Muslim's belief that the right to determine and to legislate right and wrong is reserved to God. But the fact is that there is no contradiction in this context. God's legislative prerogative was exercised in the Qur'an and the Sunna, but neither the Qur'an nor the Sunna has given, nor is expected to give, detailed laws to control every aspect of human life; it is only the general principles which may be found therein. The details are left to the discretion of the community *(umma)*, which must decide what is suitable and productive according to the circumstances. Indeed, the legislation passed by the ruler must not contradict the general principles laid down by the Qur'an and the Sunna, but when this condition is met, the ruler or rather the *umma*, is completely free to pass whatever legislation is needed.[100] This legislative right is known as *siyasa shariyya*, or governmental authority. The only condition on which this *siyasa* attains legitimacy is that it does not contradict what is contained in the Qur'an or the Sunna. According to Ibn al-Qayyim, any means which establishes justice and prevents injustice is "legitimate *siyasa*."[101]

From this review it can be said that this discretionary power (which may be the main objection of the law of *ta'zir* when expressed in words such as those quoted at the beginning of this section) is evidence of the flexibility of the Islamic penal system. Without the law of *ta'zir* the Islamic penal system would certainly have been inadequate after the first period of Islam. Within the law of *ta'zir* the Muslim state's legislative authority or, in the language of the texts, the ruler, is given the necessary power to safeguard the public interest by making harmful and disturbing behavior unlawful and prescribing punishments for it.

The jurists dealing with the subject imply that for the sake of public interest the ruler need not do this in advance. That is to say, he may punish any conduct he considers harmful to the public interest without declaring to the public that this conduct will be considered criminal.[102] This is a clear exception to the application of the general principle that no punishment can be inflicted except for an offence which has been so defined in advance. This exception allows the ruler or judge a very wide authority to punish harmful acts and omissions which may threaten the public interest in the broadest sense. Some authorities have tried to deny that granting of this discretionary power is an exception to the rule of *Nulla poena sine lege*. The argument for this view is that the *lege* exists in the general principles which command the Muslim community and the Muslim ruler to protect the public good.[103] But the fact is that these general principles are very flexible and their interpretation controversial. Consequently, one cannot agree with the above view.

It was this discretionary power which led another contemporary author to urge that *ta'zir* offenses and punishments should be codified,[104] if the Islamic penal system is to be adopted. If this view is approved, it may be through legislation that the discretionary power can be used to punish acts which threaten or harm the public interest.

However, the ruler's authority in this context is related to the Qur'anic command to the Muslim community to "enjoin what is right, and forbid what is wrong."[105] At the same time, the clear order of the Qur'an, "Obey God, His Prophet and those in authority (in charge of your affairs)" (IV:59), justifies, and was used to justify, the discretionary authority in the context of *ta'zir*.

It may be interesting to give attention to the similarity between the law of *ta'zir* and that part of the English criminal law which originated in, and is governed by, the rules of the Common Law. Here crimes and their punishments are contained in the Common Law, i.e., "the part of English law which originated in common custom and was unified and developed by the decisions and rulings of the judges."[106] Although in modern times statutes have played an increasingly important part in criminal law, there are still several crimes which exist in common law only. This means that their definitions and punishments cannot be found in an Act of Parliament but in the rulings of the judges.[107] However, several statutes prescribe specific punishments for certain common law crimes. A clear example of this is the case of murder, which remains as a common law crime while its punishment is governed by statue.[108] However, the existence of common law offences raises the question about the proper sphere of the criminal law, one aspect of which is whether it is right or wrong to grant judges a residual power to add to the criminal law.[109]

VI.   A Survey of the Law of *Ta'zir*

The ultimate objective of *ta'zir* is to punish wrong deeds which may do harm to the society or to the rights of an individual. In the first place, it is a deterrent punishment intended to prevent the commission of crimes; at the same time, it is a reformatory punishment which is intended to correct the offender. Moreover, it is the means by which a Muslim society may enforce the moral standards recommended by Islamic law. It is this last aspect, that of the enforcement of morality, which will concern us here, as enough has been said about deterrence and reformation in previous chapters.

Islamic law is essentially a code of moral standards which is to be observed in a Muslim society. The function of the various rules and obligations in Islamic law is to enforce this moral standard, even by punishment. Of the four *hada* punishments, two are concerned with sexual immorality in terms of *zina* or adultery and *qadhf* or false accusation of unchastity. The severest punishment known in Islamic law has been prescribed to enforce sexual morality.[110] Outside the field of the *hadd* punishments, the moral values of Islam are enforceable by means of *ta'zir* punishments. Examples are found in the texts (*al-Fiqh*) of acts which were considered immoral, together with their sanctions, according to the views of the jurists. But we will concentrate here on the basic issue: is it the function of the penal law to enforce the standard of conventional morality by punishing deviation from it?[111]

The problem of law and morality, particularly sexual morality, has been the subject of a lively discussion among lawyers and philosophers in England. It follows the famous decision of the House of Lords in the case of *Shaw v. the Director of Public Prosecutions* in 1961. Mr. Shaw had published a magazine entitled *The Ladies' Directory,* which listed the names and addresses of prostitutes and included some photographs and indications of their particular sexual practices. The House of Lords dismissed Mr. Shaw's appeal against conviction for three offences, one of which was "conspiring to corrupt public morals." The formulation, or re-formulation, of this offence by the English law, stimulated a debate concerning the relationship between law and morality.[112] It is interesting that the debate on this issue is expected to attract lawyers and philosophers again after two recent cases. The first is the case of the *Director of Public Prosecutions v. Richard Neville and others.* This is the case known as the "OZ" case. Mr. Neville and two of his colleagues published Number 28 of the *OZ Magazine* entitled *School Kids' OZ.* They were convicted by the Central Criminal Court of 28 July, 1971, and sentenced on 5 August, 1971, (Judge Argyle, Q.C.) to fifteen, twelve and nine months imprisonment, respectively.   The Court of Appeal suspended the sentences on 5 November, 1971. In this case the conviction was made according to the Obscene Publications Act, 1959, and the Post Office Act, 1953. But the three men were acquitted of conspiracy to corrupt public morals.

The second case is that of the *Director of Public Prosecution v. Stage I (Publishing Company).* This publishing company brought out a book entitled *The Little Red School-Book.* It aimed at informing school children about almost everything in life. The section on sex (twenty-six pages) was declared obscene by the magistrate, Mr. John Denis Purcell on 1 July, 1971. The court based its verdict on the grounds that this section was likely to "deprave and corrupt" young people. The publishing company appealed against the court's decision but the appeal was dismissed.[113]

There are two views concerning the role of law in the enforcement of morals among British lawyers. The first view was held by the English Lords, as expressed in their decision in the *Shaw* case, and defended by some writers afterward.[114] According to this view, criminal law must enforce public morality or the accepted standard of morals. Lord Patrick Devlin, in his book, *The Enforcement of Morals,* supported this view very strongly. It is admitted, according to some, that the morality which the law presupposes is not beyond criticism and should be subject to informed discussion and debate.[115] This view was criticized by those who hold that the law ought not to interfere with private morality, and the criticism is from both the moral and legal points of view.[116]

Islamic law, on the other hand, presents a view according to which no distinction may be made between private and public morality. It is true that the standard of proof required to establish the offence of adultery by testimony, for example, would certainly mean that the offender had committed an offence of public indecency, even under English Law.[117] But when the offender commits such an offence in private, he is expected to repent although he is not brought before a court. This concept of repentance *(tawbah)* means that an immoral sexual act, even in private, amounts to a sin for which the offender must repent or he will be punished in the hereafter.[118] Such a concept is the outgrowth of the religious nature of Islamic law, with which the court has nothing to do, and which is not relevant to secular law. However, examples may be easily found in the texts of acts which would merely be considered immoral in a secular state, while they are considered offences of *ta'zir* under Islamic law. Although there is no clear distinction in the Qur'an between moral and legal rules, since Qur'anic precepts merely indicate the standards of conduct which are acceptable or unacceptable to God,[119] every unacceptable act is *"ma'siya"* or "corruption" for which a *ta'zir* punishment may be imposed. And when the transgression is committed in circumstances which cannot justify the court's intervention, the offender is always obliged to repent in order to escape punishment in the next life. This concept of repentance is, by nature, a process of self-reformation which is assumed to serve the same purpose as the *ta'zir* punishment. It can accordingly be said that among the purposes of the *ta'zir* punishment is the enforcement of the standard of morals approved by Islamic law, in terms of its punishing immoral or morally-disapproved conduct.

Ta'zir punishments, therefore, must differ in each case, as has been said, in consideration of the offender, the crime, and the victim, when possible. For this reason some jurists have classified offenders, or rather citizens, into four distinct classes: (1) the most distinguished of the upper classes, i.e., officials and officers of the highest rank, for whom a personal communication from the judge through a confidential messenger would suffice as a penalty; (2) the upper classes, i.e., the intellectual elite and scholars of the Shari'a, who may be summoned before the judge and admonished by him; (3) the middle classes, i.e., the merchants, who should be punished by imprisonment, and (4) the lower strata of the people who should be punished by imprisonment or flogging.[120] Other jurists, however, reject this external classification according to social status and lay stress on the inner worth of the individual, his attitude toward religion, and his mode of life.[121]

A final question which may be asked about ta'zir as a reformatory punishment is how it can be so considered when it imposes the death penalty or flogging, which are mainly deterrent punishments, as has been previously observed. Here it must be noted that the reformatory function appears in the deterrence value of these punishments, which is supposed to result in the prevention of further similar crimes. It is also necessary to allow such punishments to be used as ta'zir because, to use Lord Simond's words, "no one can foresee every way in which the wickedness of man may disrupt the order of society."[122]

Now, to conclude, one can say that the law of ta'zir provides Muslim states in modern times with the principles according to which they can formulate, outside the limited area of the hadd punishments, modern penal codes to be applied by the courts adopting modern systems of law. The variety of punishments allowed as ta'zir can save the modern Muslim states from having to borrow their penal laws from Western models, as has happened in most of the Arab countries. At the same time, for those who demand the application of Islamic criminal law, there is no better course than to concentrate on exemplifying the law of ta'zir as the best proof of their claim that the Islamic concept of punishment is valid and can be adopted in modern times.

NOTES

1. *Mukhtar al-Sihah*, under *'azr*; *'Amer al-Ta'zir*, p. 36.
2. Qur'an v:12, VII:157, and XLVIII:9.
3. Ibn Farhun, *Tabsirah*, vol. II, p. 200.
4. Sarakhsi, *Mabsut*, vol. IX, p. 36; Shirbini, *Mughni al-Muhtaj*, vol. IV, p. 176.
5. Ibn Nujaym, *Al-Bahr al-Ra'iq Sharh Kanz al-Daqa'iq*, vol. V, p. 44 ff.; Ibn al-Humam *Fath, al-Qadir*, vol. IV, p. 211 ff.
6. *Encyclopaedia of Islam*, vol. IV, p. 710, under *"Ta'zir"*.
7. IV:16.
8. Ibn Kathir, *Tafsir*, vol. I, p. 462; Sayed Qutb, *Fi-Zilal al-Quran*, vol. IV, p. 257 Ibn al-Jawzi, *Zad al-Masir fi 'Ilm al-Tafsir*, vol. II, p. 34.
9. IV:34.
10. Concerning the husbans's authority over the family or rather the wife, the Qur'a says, "Men are in charge of women, because God has made the one of them tc excel the other" (IV:34).
11. *Mughni al-Muhtaj*, p. 176.
12. The beginning of XLII:40.
13. The latter part of XLII:40.
14. See Ibn al-Qayyim, *Ighathat al-Lahfan*, vol. I, p. 333; Shalabi, *Ta'lil al-Ahkam* pp. 60–61, in relation to drinking.
15. Ibn al-Qayyim, op. cit., p. 332. This *hadith* was transmitted by Ahmad b. Hanbal Abu-Dawud and Ibn Majah.
16. Ibid.; *I'lam al-Muwaqq'in*, vol. II, p. 98.
17. IX:118.
18. Ibn al-Qayyim, *Zad al-Ma'ad*, vol. III, pp. 11–13. See also *Ighathat al-Lahfan*, p 332.
19. *Mishkat al-Masabih*, vol. II, p. 146, and Ibn al-Qayyim, op. cit.
20. Ibn al-Qayyim, op. cit., p. 331.
21. *Mishkat al-Masabih*, p. 112.
22. I have omitted many other reports relating to the subject because it may be argued tha they were invented by the jurists to support one or another of the different view concerning this punishment.
23. Compare the article on *"Ta'zir"* in the *Encyclopaedia of Islam*, vol. IV.
24. Ibn Nujaym, *Al-Bahr al-Ra'iq*, vol. V, p. 44; 'Uda, op. cit., vol. I, pp. 685–708
25. 'Uda, op. cit. p. 143.
26. Ibid., p. 687.
27. Qarafi, *Furuq*, vol. IV, pp. 179–180.
28. 'Amer, *Al-Ta'zir*, op. cit., p. 369, where Ibn 'Abdin is quoted.
29. 'Uda, op. cit., p. 702.
30. *Mishkat al-Masabih*, vol. II, p. 586, where Bayhaqi in *Shu'ab al-Iman* is quoted
31. 'Uda, op. cit., p. 703.
32. Cross and Jones, *Introduction to Criminal Law*, p. 354; *The Sentence of the Court a Handbook for Courts on the Treatment of Offenders*, H.M.S.O., London, 197C
33. See above, and Muslim, op. cit., vol. VIII, p. 106; Ibn-Taymiyya, *Al-Siyasa' al Shar'iya'*, pp. 120–121.
34. Ibn Farhun, *Tabsirat al-Hukkam*, p. 202.
35. 'Amer, op. cit., p. 375.
36. *Mishkat al-Masabih*, vol. I, p. 560.
37. Sarakhsi, *Mabsut*, vol. 16, p. 145.

38. Bahuti, *Kashshaf al-Qina'*, vol. VI, p. 125; Shirbini, *Mughni al-Muhtaj*, vol. IV, p. 178; Ibn Farhun, op. cit., p. 214.
39. Ibn Farhun, op. cit.
40. Bahuti, op. cit. pp. 127–128; Sarakhsi, op. cit., p. 145 ff.; 'Amer, op. cit. pp. 388-419.
41. Ibn Nujaym, *Al-Bahr al-Ra'iq*, vol. V, p. 44; Ibn al-Humam, *Fath al-Qadir*, vol. IV, p. 212; Shubramulsi's commentary on *Sharh al-Minhaj* by al-Ramli, vol. VII, p. 174.
42. Shubramulsi, op. cit.; Ibn 'Abdin, op. cit., vol. IV, p. 61; Ibn Farhun, op. cit., p. 203; Ibn al-Qayyim, *Al-Turuq al-Hukmiyya*, pp. 286-290; Bahuti, op. cit., vol. VI, p. 125. Cf. *Fath al-Qadir*.
43. Ibn Nujaym, op. cit., vol. IV, p. 44; Ibn 'Abdin, op. cit., vol. IV, p. 61; Sa'di Jelbi's commentary on *Al-'Inaya Sharh al-Hidaya* in the margin of *Fath al-Qadir*, vol. IV, p. 212.
44. Jelbi, op. cit.
45. Ibid., p. 212, Ibn Nujayn, op. cit., p. 44; Ibn 'Abdin, op. cit.
46. Ibn Taymiyya, *Al-Hisba fi'l-Islam*, p. 43; Ibn al-Qayyim, *Al-Turuq al-Hukmiyya*, pp. 286-290; *Ighathat al-Lahfan*, vol. I, pp. 231-233. A detailed discussion may be found in 'Amer, *Al-Ta'zir*, pp. 331-336.
47. *Al-Turuq al-Hukmiyya*, pp. 287-288.
48. Ibn-Farhun, *Tabsirah*, vol. II, pp. 202-203; Bahuti, op. cit., p. 125; Tarabulsi, *Mu'in al-Hukkam*, p. 190.
49. J. Schacht, *An Introduction to Islamic Law*, p. 176; cf. Shaltut, *Al-Islam*, p. 314.
50. 'Uda, op. cit., vol. I, p. 694.
51. *Mughni*, vol. X, pp. 347-348. Ibn Farhun, op. cit., p. 225.
52. Ibn Farhun, op. cit.; Abu Ya'la, *Al-Ahkam al-Sultaniya*, p. 263; *Al-Durr al-Mukhtar*, in the margin of *Hashiyat Ibn 'Abdin*, vol. IV, p. 62.
53. *Tabsirat al-Hukkam*, p. 225; 'Uda, op. cit., pp. 694-695; 'Amer, op. cit., pp. 309-310.
54. This view was ascribed to Mawardi and Ramli; see the references cited above.
55. *Fath al-Qadir*, vol. IV, p. 216; AbuYa'la, op. cit., p. 267; Ibn Farhun, op. cit., pp. 225-226; Ansari, *Sharh Rawd al-Talib*, vol. IV, p. 199.
56. Ibn 'Abdin, op. cit., p. 67; Ibn Farhun, op. cit., p. 227; Bahutti, *Kashshaf al-Qina*, vol. VI, p. 126; Ramli, *Nihayat al-Muhtaj*, vol. VIII, p. 272.
57. See Ramli, op. cit.
58. See above chapter on *hadd* punishment.
59. AbuYa'la, op. cit., p. 263; Ibn Farhun, op. cit., p. 225.
60. 'Uda, op. cit., pp. 699-700.
61. Ibn Farhun, op. cit., pp. 204-205; Zurqani's commentary on *Mukhtasar Khalil*, vol. VIII, p. 143.
62. *Muhalla*, vol. XI, p. 404; *Al-Rawd al-Nadir*, vol. IV, p. 178; Ibn al-Qayyim, *Al-Turuq al-Hukmiyya*, p. 116, where some Hanbali scholars who hold this view are mentioned.
63. 'Uda, op. cit., pp. 690-693; Ibn al-Qayyim, op. cit.; *Muhalla*, pp. 401–402.
64. *Mishkat al-Masabih*, vol. II, p. 310; Zubaydi, *Al-Tajrid al-Sarih*, vol. II, p. 151; Mundhiri, *Mukhtasar Sahih Muslim*, with the commentary of Albani, vol. II, p. 39.
65. Bayhaqi, *Al-Sunan al-Kubra*, vol. VIII, p. 327.
66. *Fath al-Qadir*, vol. IV, p. 215; 'Uda, op. cit., vol. I, p. 692; Ibn Farhun, op. cit., vol. II, p. 204.
67. Ibn Taymiyya, *Al-Siyasa al-Shar'iya*, p. 125; Ibn al-Qayyim, *I'lam al-Muwaqq'in*,

vol. II, pp. 29-30. This view is also held by Ibn al-Shat, a Maliki scholar; see his commentary on Qarafi's *Furuq*, vol. IV, p. 177.

68. For example, Shawkani, *Nayl al-Awtar*, vol. VII, pp. 150-151.
69. That is, a Prophetic report or *hadith* resting on a chain of authorities that goes no further back than the second generation after the Prophet. The validity of establishing a legal obligation on the basis of this kind of *hadith* is controversial. See Shafi'i, *Al-Risala*, p. 465; Ibn Kathir, *Mukhtasar 'Ulum al-Hadith*, with the commentary of Ahmad Shakir, pp. 37-41; Ibn Hazm, *Al-Ihkam fi' Usul al-Ahkam*, vol. II, pp. 2–6; Naysaburi, *Ma'rifat 'Ulum al-Hadith*, with the commentary of Dr. Muzzam Husain, pp. 25-27.
70. 'Uda, op. cit., vol. I, pp. 692–693, where the various interpretations of this hadith are discussed.
71. *Fath al-Qadir*, p. 215; Ibn 'Abdin, vol. IV, p. 60.
72. Ibn Nujaym, *Al-Ashbah wal-Naza'ir*, vol. I, p. 168 ff.
73. Ibn Farhun, op. cit., vol. II, p. 205; Kinani, *Al-'Iqd al-Munazzam*, in the margin of *Tabsirat al-Hukkam*, vol. II, p. 266; Bahuti, op. cit., vol. VI, p. 124; Ibn 'Abdin, op. cit., vol. IV, p. 63.
74. Ibn 'Abdin, op. cit., pp. 27, 62–64; Ibn Nujaym, *Al-Bahr al-Ra'iq*, vol. V, p. 45.
75. Quoted from Prof. Coulson's article, "The State and the Individual in Islamic Law," *International and Comparative Law Quarterly*, January 1957, vol. VI, p. 54. See also Ibn Farhun, op. cit., vol. II, p. 200 ff.
76. Ibn al-Qayyim, *Al-Turuq al-Hukmiyya*, p. 286; Bahuti, op.cit. p. 126; *Matalib Uli al-Nuha*, vol. VI, p. 224.
77. See above, chapter II, and Ibn al-Qayyim, *Zad al-Ma'ad*, vol. II, p. 68.
78. 'Uda, op. cit., vol. I, p. 688.
79. Coulson, op. cit., p. 53.
80. For example, V:95, VI:160, X:27, XL:40, XLII:40.
81. *Al-Sarim al-Maslul*, p. 12. It was quoted by some Hanifi authorities as their own school's view, e.g., Ibn 'Abdin, op. cit., vol. IV, pp. 62-63, 214-215, where he confirms that what Ibn Taymiyya said is the Hanafi school's view.
82. For the doctrine of "*siyasa*" see Coulson, "The State and the Individual," *International and Comparative Law Quarterly*, vol. VI, Jan. 1957, pp. 51–52; *A History of Islamic Law*, pp. 132–134, 184–185; and *Conflicts and Tensions in Islamic Jurisprudence*, pp. 68–69. Cf. Cherif Bassiouni, "Islam Concept, Law and World Habeas Corpus," *Camden Law Journal*, vol. 7, no. 2, 1969.
83. Ibn Farhun, op. cit., vol. II, p. 159; *Mawahib al-Jalil*, a commentary on *Mukhtasar Khalil*, vol. VI, p. 247.
84. 'Amer, *Al-Ta'zir*, pp. 243–248.
85. Shaltut, *Al-Islam 'Aqida wa Shari'a*, p. 314.
86. Coulson, "The State and the Individual," op. cit., p. 53.
87. Al-Qarafi, *Furuq*, vol. III, pp. 16–20.
88. Ibid., vol. IV, p. 182, translated in Prof. Coulson's article, op. cit.
89. Ibid, p. 182.
90. Shalabi, *Al-Fiqh al-Islami*, p. 42. 'Uda, op. cit., vol. I, pp. 223–237. The Qur'an stresses this principle in various chapters, e.g., V:48; VI:57, 62; XII:40, 67; XVIII: 26; XLII: 21.
91. IV:135, XXII:30, XXV:72.
92. IV:58 and VIII:27. To prove the criminal nature of breach of trusts, some writers have referred to XXXIII:72, but this verse is irrelevant to this subject. There the word "*amanah*" means responsibility to God, while in the verses quoted it means financial trust. Cf. 'Uda, op. cit. vol. I, p. 139.

93. XLIX:11.
94. II:188.
95. For other examples, and for reports concerned with the five examples given above, see 'Uda, op. cit. pp. 138–143.
96. Shatibi, *Muwafaqat*, vol. I, p. 38, and vol. II, p. 10.
97. Ibn Farhun, op. cit., vol. II, p. 106; see also Coulson, op. cit., p. 51.
98. For example, II:190, III:104, 110 and 114, and XXII:41.
99. Shatibi, *Muwafaqat*, vol. II, pp. 7–14. Shalabi, *Al-Fiqh al-Islami*, pp. 110–112.
100. Qarafi, *Ihkam*, pp. 26–31.
101. *Al-Turuq al-Hukmiyya*, pp. 14–20. The same view was supported by Ibn-Farhun, op. cit., p. 104, and Tarabulsi's *Mu'in al-Hukkam*, p. 164.
102. 'Uda, op. cit., vol. I, pp. 150–152.
103. Ibid., pp. 152–154.
104. 'Amer, *Al-Ta'zir*, pp. 404–408.
105. Ibn 'Abdin, *Minhat al-Khaliq*, a commentary on *Al-Bahr al-Ra'iq of Ibn Nujaym*, vol. VI, p. 45; Ibn Nujaym, *Risalah fi Iqamat al-Qadi al-Ta'zir*, supplemented to his *Ashbah wa-Naza'ir*, vol. II, pp. 46–48.
106. Cross and Jones, *Introduction to Criminal Law*, p. 16.
107. Ibid., p. 17.
108. Until 1965 it was punished by the death penalty, which was then abolished for murder by the 1965 Abolition of Death Penalty Act.
109. See Cross and Jones, op.cit., pp. 18–21. This question was recently discussed after the House of Lords' decision in the case of *Shaw v. Director of Public Prosecution* (1961), to which we will refer shortly.
110. See above, chapter I.
111. A discussion of the subject is found in Coulson, *Conflicts and Tensions*, pp. 77 ff.
112. See H.L.A. Hart, *Law, Liberty and Morality*, pp. 6–12; Coulson, op. cit., p. 77; B. Mitchell, *Law, Morality and Religion in a Secular Society*, pp. 12, 61. For a general discussion of the subject, see Lord Patrick Devlin, *The Enforcement of Morals*.
113. For both cases see *The Times*, July 2, Aug. 6 and 9, and Nov. 6, 1971.
114. E.g., A.L. Goodhart, *The Shaw Case: The Law and Public Morals, Law Quarterly Review*, vol. 77, 1961, p. 567, and B. Mitchell, op. cit., pp. 134-135.
115. Mitchell, *op. cit.*
116. Hart, H.L.A., *The Morality of the Criminal Law*. Cf. Abrahams, G., *Morality and the Law*, pp. 84–127; Fuller, L.L., *The Morality of Law*, chaps. 2 and 3, and his criticism of Professor Hart's view, chap. 5.
117. Coulson, op. cit., p. 78.
118. Coulson, op. cit., p. 80.
119. Shalabi, *Al-Fiqh al-Islami*, pp. 24–32; Shaltut, op. cit., p. 459.
120. Kasani, *Badai' al-Sanai'*, vol. VII, p. 64; *Encyclopaedia of Islam*, vol. IV, p. 710.
121. Ibn 'Abdin, *Hashiya*, p. 62; also *Encyclopaedia of Islam*.
122. Hart, *Law, Liberty and Morality*, p. 9.

CHAPTER V

The Law of Evidence In Criminal Cases

I. Introduction

The relationship between the infliction of punishment and the evidence required to prove crimes is a very clear one. Where the court is not absolutely certain of the guilt of the accused, the punishment cannot be inflicted. Methods of proof in any penal system reflect the legislator's desire to widen or limit the number of cases in which a particular punishment may or may not be inflicted. Hence a brief account of the law of evidence in criminal cases under the Islamic penal system will help us to form a more precise image of the theory of punishment in Islamic law.

The aim of the law of evidence in Islamic legal theory in general was rightly described as "the establishment of the truth of claims with a high degree of certainty."[1] Thus, the usual evidence is the oral testimony of two adult Muslims who must be known to the judge as having the highest degree of moral and religious probity (*'adala*). This common standard of proof should be, as a general rule, complied with in all criminal and civil cases. However, there are some recognized alternatives to it in both civil and criminal procedures. The alternative methods of proof in criminal cases which will be dealt with here are the criminal's admission or confession *(iqrar)*, the judge's personal observation *('ilm al-qadi)*, and circumstantial evidence *(al-qara'in)*. The pre-Islamic method of proof in cases of homicide known as oath *(qasamah)* will not be dealt with in this context as I do not see it as a recognized system under Islamic law.[2] The most important exception to the ordinary standard of proof in criminal cases is that of requiring four male witnesses to prove the offence of adultery or fornication *(zina)*. Hence, this will be treated separately.

II. Testimony *(Shahada):*

Most criminal charges are to be proved by the oral testimony of two adult male Muslims. Among *hadd* crimes, this rule applies to the crimes of *sariqa qadhf* and *hiraba,* and it also applies to the most serious *ta'zir* offences, i.e., drinking and apostasy.[3] *Qisas* for crimes of homicide cannot be applied unless the crime is proved in the same manner. The Maliki school differentiates only between *qisas* for homicide and for injuries, and relaxes the rule of the two male witnesses for the latter by allowing it to be proved by the testimony of one witness and the oath of the victim, or one male and two female witnesses.[4] It is clear, then, that the jurists pay a good deal of attention to the evidence of the witnesses and to when it can be accepted. The most important part of their discussion is concerned with the witnesses' characters or the condition of *'adala.*

The origin of the condition of *'adala* is the Qur'anic injunction," . . . and call to witness two just men . . .''[5] Differences among the schools of Islamic law about what is meant by *'adala* are generally of little importance. Nevertheless, some are worth mentioning. The Hanafi, Maliki, and Shafi'i' schools consider a Muslim *'adl* if he usually does what is required of him and avoids doing what is forbidden. The Hanbali jurists add to this what they call *isti' mal al-muru'ah,* or a sense of honor. This was explained by a Hanbali jurist as meaning the avoidance of what takes away a person's respectability and the upholding of what makes him respectable.[7]

The Zahiri school holds that a person is *'adl* if he is not known to have committed any serious crime or grave offence *(kabira),* and has not openly committed a venial sin *(saghira).*[8]   · *kabira* they mean what the Prophet termed "*kabira,*" and that for which there is the threat of punishment in the Qur'an or the Sunna.[9] Ibn Hazm supported this view by quoting the Qur'anic verse, "If you avoid the great sins which are forbidden, we will remit from you your evil deds. . .''[10] He says that according to this verse everything is remissable as long as a Muslim does not commit any great sin *(kabira).* What is remissable in the judgment of God, Ibn Hazm continued, cannot incur blame or reprimand on its perpetrator. At the same time, anyone who commits *kabira* and afterwards repents should be considered *'adl,* as though he had never committed it.[11]

It is interesting to note that the schools of Islamic law are divided on the question of whether a Muslim should be considered *'adl* unless proven not to be, or whether he should not be considered *adl* until his *'adala* is proven. The first view is held by the Zahiri and Hanafi schools, while the second is held by the Maliki, Shafi'i, Hanbali, and Zaydi schools.[12]

Finally, it is noteworthy that Ibn al-Qayyim and his teacher, Ibn Taymiyya, hold that all criminal and civil claims can be proven by the testimony of one witness if the judge is satisfied that he is telling the truth. The only exception to this procedure is in the case of crimes for which there are *hadd* punishments; these crimes are to be testified to by two male witnesses except in the case of *zina*, for which four are required.[13]

II. 1. Testimony in Cases of *Zina*

The evidence required in cases of *zina* is the oral testimony of four adult male Muslims who have seen the actual act of sexual intercourse. This is derived from the Qur'anic verse, "As for those of your women who are guilty of lewdness, call to witness four of you against them."[14] All jurists agree on the number of witnesses and their sex. Women's testimony is not accepted in cases of adultery or in any *hadd* offence.[15] The witnesses must be able to state where and when the offence took place, and must be able to identify the party to the act. Testimony, moreover, must be delivered before the court in one sitting *(fi-majlisin wahid)*.[16]

The punishment for *qadhf* is inflicted on the above witnesses if they are less than four. Accordingly, if four people witnessed the act but only three of them are prepared to give testimony before the court, they can be convicted of the offence of *qadhf* and punished accordingly, regardless of the reasons which prevented the fourth from giving his testimony.[17]

These requirements indicate the difficulty, if not the impossibility, of inflicting the *hadd* punishment for fornication or adultery. Some jurists have expressed the view that the deterrent effect of punishment in Islamic law is demonstrated by the fact that these punishments are theoretically prescribed but not actually inflicted. And this is as true for the rest of the *hadd* punishments as it is for *zina*.[18] The severity of punishment in Islamic law indicates the law-maker's desire to warn the people in order to prevent them from committing the offences in question, while the obvious difficulty of proving the offence reflects his desire to regard the existence of these punishments as a mere threat. The fact that we can cite no case throughout Islamic history in which the crime of *zina* was established through testimony is very significant. It must be noted, however, that it is not only the number of witnesses required which makes it difficult to prove adultery or fornication, but also the threat of being punished for *qadhf* if the witnesses fail to agree on every minute detail. Practically speaking, no one would risk giving testimony when he could expect to be punished if one of the witnesses, did not testify for any reason, or if the statements of the four differed in any way.

III. Confession *(Iqrar)*

An alternative method of proof in criminal cases which we will examine here is the establishment of proof by the criminal's own confession *(iqrar)*. It is agreed that the criminal's confession is sufficient for the establishment of his guilt and that, on the basis of his confession, the appropriate punishment can be inflicted. A single confession is sufficient in all criminal cases other than *zina*, concerning which the necessary number of confessions is disputed. According to the Hanafi, Hanbali, and Zaydi schools, the confession of *zina* must be repeated four times since the minimum number of witnesses in such a case is four, and because of the case of Ma'iz who confessed adultery four times to the Prophet. It was only after the fourth confession that the Prophet started his inquiry into the truthfulness of his confession, his state of mind, and his awareness of the punishment for the act.[19]

The Maliki, Shafi'i, and Zahiri schools disagree with this view and hold that one confession is sufficient to establish the confessor's guilt. They see a difference between testimony and confession. The former rests on the mere assumption that the witnesses are telling the truth; consequently, a large number of witnesses are necessary in order to avoid any possibility of false testimony. The latter rests on the confessor's own volition; hence there cannot be any shadow of doubt as to its credibility. Moreover, they cite another *hadith* in which the Prophet did not require the confession to be repeated.[20]

The Zaydis, on the other hand, hold that the point of requiring the confession to be repeated four times is to give the confessor an opportunity to withdraw his confession and escape the *hadd* punishment by repentance, which is a recommended practice.[21]

Apart from this dispute concerning *zina* among the different schools, another dispute exists within the Hanafi school itself. In cases of *qadhf*, theft, and drinking, Abu Yusuf, the second founder of the school, holds that a confession must be repeated twice, although the imam, Abu Hanifa, himself did not require the repetition of the confession. Abu Yusuf based his view on the fact that the punishment of these crimes is the right of

God (*haqq Allah*), and so it can be inflicted only after the taking of all possible precautions (*ihtiyat*), while Abu Hanifa held that confession is the communication of a piece of news (*ikhbar*) which cannot be strengthened by repetition. The difference between such crimes and *zina* is that the four confessions required for the latter derive from the Prophet's practice, while nothing similar exists concerning any of the other *hadd* crimes.[22] Analogy (*qiyas*), a Hanafi jurist stated, cannot help Abu Yusuf to prove his view because it is not applicable in such cases.[23]

Confession should be made in detail, showing that the confessor is aware of what he has done and proving that his action was in fact the crime for which a punishment is prescribed. If a summarized confession were acceptable, someone might confess that he had, for example, committed *zina* while he actually had not, resulting in his being punished unjustly. Accordingly, a detailed confession is required and it is the judge's duty to ask the confessor about the minute details of his offence.[24] Associated with this principle is the rule that a confession must be made in clear and explicit words since an indirect confession, i.e., by way of *kinaya*, is not accepted as proof in criminal cases.[25] Hence, the Hanifi school does not accept the confession of a mute person even if he makes it in writing, because they consider writing as an indirect declaration, although the other Sunni schools disagree with this view and accept the mute individual's confession as long as his signs or his writing are intelligible.[26]

A confession in criminal, but not in civil, cases can be withdrawn even after sentence has been passed or during its execution. In cases of its withdrawal after sentencing, a *hadd* punishment should no longer be carried out, although a *ta'zir* punishment may be imposed even after the withdrawal of the confession. The reason is that the withdrawal of the confession causes doubt (*shubha*), rendering the *hadd* punishment nonapplicable, but this rule does not apply with regard to *ta'zir*.[27] Moreover, it is recommended to judges that if someone confesses to having committed a crime considered as *haqq Allah*, he should be given a chance to withdraw his confession. This recommendation is based on the fact that in such cases the criminal's repentance is better than his punishment.[28]

In all cases the confession applies only to the confessor. Accordingly, when a man confesses that he and another man have been drinking but the alleged participant denies it, only the confessor can be punished. In cases in which the crime cannot have been committed by a single person alone, e.g., *zina*, the schools of Islamic law are divided as to the authority of one partner's confession when the other denies the alleged crime. The Hanbal and Shafi'i schools hold that the confessor should be punished according to his confession regardless of the other person's denial, and the same view is held by Abu Yusuf and Muhammad b. al-Hassan (the two companions of Abu Hanifa).[29] According to Abu Hanifa, if the alleged partner in such a crime denies the allegation, neither of the two partners can be punished. He holds that since such a crime cannot be committed except by two people, if the act of one of them is not proved, then the role of the other is not definitely established; hence it would neither be just to punish the confessor and leave the other party unpunished nor to punish them both. Logically, this view seems more acceptable than the former, since the partner's denial sheds doubt on the correctness of the confessor's statement, and, as we saw, *hadd* punishments are not to be inflicted when there is any sort of doubt, however little.[30]

With such conditions required for a valid confession, and with the possibility of its withdrawal at any stage, even after the beginning of the carrying out of the sentence, one can say that confession in criminal cases has a very limited role as a method of proof. This fact is especially true when we consider the severity of the *hadd* punishments, which might prevent even the most pious person from confessing his guilt. Evidence of this view is that since the Kingdom of Saudi Arabia revived the application of the Islamic criminal law more than fifty years ago, only one case of *zina* is known to have been proved by confession.[31]

IV. The Judge's Personal Observation *('Ilm al-Qadi)*

The Zahiri school is the only one which allows a judge to formulate judgments according to his own observation in all criminal cases. Ibn Hazm in his famous text, *Al Muhalla,* stated: "It is obligatory *(fard)* for the judge to give judgments according to his personal observation in all civil and criminal cases . . . the fairest judgment is that which is based on the judge's personal observation, then on the defendant's confession, then on testimony." Ibn Hazm defended this view by relating the task of the judiciary to the duty of "enjoining what is right and forbidding what is wrong;" this is a duty on every Muslim and the judge is no exception to this rule.[32]

The Hanafi, Maliki, and Hanbali schools forbid the judge to give judgment according to his personal observation in all criminal cases (with the exception of *ta'zir* cases, according to some), holding that he cannot act except according to the evidence delivered before him; his own observations are no more valuable than those of any single witness. At the same time, the judge is not allowed to add his own testimony to that of other witnesses in order to complete the number of witnesses required in a given case, because it is impossible to be a judge and a witness at the same time.[33] The two views are said to be held by the Shafi'i school, but the majority of the Shafi'i scholars in fact hold the latter.[34] The majority view was defended by Ibn al—Qayyim who supported it by citing some Prophetic reports and views attributed to the Companions of the Prophet.[35]

The Zaydi school makes a distinction between cases of *qisas* and *qadhf*, in which the judge is allowed to act on his own knowledge, and other criminal cases, in which he is not allowed to do so. Such a distinction is unknown to the other schools, who either allow it in all cases or in none. Moreover, one cannot find any logic in it or any sound argument for its validity.[36]

Based on the foregoing, one can say that the Zahiri view seems to contradict the principles laid down in the Qur'an and Sunna in relation to methods of proof. While the Qur'an requires four adult male witnesses to establish guilt in cases of *zina*, the Zahiris allow it to be established by only one witness if he happens to be the judge. Thus the relationship between the Qur'anic command to enjoin the right and forbid the wrong and the judge's duty may be interpreted in an entirely different manner; that is to say, it is "wrong" to pass judgments without the evidence required by the law. Accordingly, the majority view is the most convincing one, as neither the Zahiris' nor the Zaydis' view is valid.

V.   Circumstantial Evidence *(al-Qara'in)*

The generally accepted view is that circumstantial evidence *(qara'in)* is not one of the methods of proof recognized under Islamic law. At the same time, some jurists consider circumstantial evidence as an acceptable means of proof in the absence of others. Ibn al-Qayyim and the Maliki scholar, Ibn Farhun, are the two main representatives of this view.

Circumstantial evidence is a valid method of proof, according to the above authorities, in all civil and criminal cases except *hadd* offences, though the offence of *zina* may be proved against an unmarried woman if she is pregnant.[37] There are other examples of criminal cases for which circumstantial evidence may be sufficient proof. Drinking, for example, may be proved by the smell of the breath of the accused or on his vomiting alcohol, a rule which is associated with 'Omar and Ibn Masu'd, the Companions of the Prophet.[38] In cases of *qisas*, circumstantial evidence is sufficient when a man runs out of a house with a knife in his hand, a man bleeding to death is immediately found there, and there is no sign of any other possible assailant; in such a case the fleeing man is obviously the killer.[39] In a similar case, the Chief Alkali of Bida, Northern Nigeria, commented that this evidence was "better than testimony."[40]

The procedure of *qasama,* again in the context of *qisas*, is a good example of circumstantial evidence being considered a justification for the swearing of oaths and inflicting *qisas* or exacting *diya*.[41]

The Ibadi school, usually referred to as a part of the Khariji sect,[42] considers that *qara'in* is proper evidence in cases of homicide. This view is based on a *hadith* according to which the Prophet gave the booty of a murdered man, after the battle of Badr, to a member of the Muslim army because of circumstantial evidence that he had killed the enemy.[43] To this view some contemporary scholars give a good deal of credence.[44] However, this view has not traditionally been supported, since the Sunni schools generally hold to the testimony of two male witnesses.

The arguments put forward by Ibn al-Qayyim and Ibn Farhun may at least dispel the notion that Islamic law does not recognize circumstantial evidence in its formulation of the law of evidence.[45] But where circumstantial evidence is the only method of proof available, the court must take all possible precautions to avoid injustice or misjudgment.[46] When definite evidence is almost impossible, writes one Hanafi jurist, the nearest to it must be accepted.[47]

It is interesting that according to Qarafi, the famous Maliki jurist, circumstantial evidence may be considered only by the court of the *wali al-jara'im*, or the official in charge of crimes. But another Maliki authority, Ibn Farhun, considers that the ordinary Shari'a court or the *qadi* may also take circumstantial evidence into consideration.[48] Here it seems that the latter authority was influenced by the very strong argument of Ibn al-Qayyim and by his conclusion that the final purpose of the law of God is to establish justice among people; therefore whatever means need to be employed for this are legitimate.[49]

In this chapter I have intentionally avoided any comparison between Islamic law and modern penal systems because such a comparison in this particular context would not make any significant contribution to the subject, let alone be of any practical importance.

NOTES

1. Coulson, *A History of Islamic Law,* p. 126.
2. For details, see Ahmad Ibrahim, *Al-Qisas,* pp. 228–235, where a similar view is expressed.
3. Ibn Farhun, *Tabsirah,* vol. I, p. 212–213.
4. Ibid., p. 215; 'Uda, op. cit., vol. II, p. 316; Baji, *Muntaqa,* vol. V, p. 215.
5. LXV:2
6. *Mabsut,* vol. XVI, p. 121; *Muntaqa,* vol. V, p. 195; Bajirmi, *Tuhfat al-Habib 'ala Sharh al-Khatib,* vol. IV, p. 339 ff.
7. Hajawi, *Matn al-Iqna',* published with Bahuti, *Kashshaf al-Qina',* vol. VI, p. 422. See also *Mughni,* vol. X, p. 149.
8. *Muhalla,* vol. IX, p. 393 ff.
9. Ibid. See also Qarafi, *Furuq,* vol. IV, pp. 66–70.
10. IV:31.
11. See *Muhalla.*
12. *Muhalla;* Baji, op. cit., p. 193; 'Uda, op. cit., vol. II, pp. 404–405.
13. Ibn al-Qayyim, *Al-Turuq al-Hukmiyya,* p. 73, 77, 82 and 176–178.
14. IV:15.
15. *Mughni,* vol. IX, pp. 69–70.
16. Ibid., p. 71; Kasani, *Badai',* vol. VII, p. 48; Ibn-Farhun, *Tabsirah,* vol. I, p. 212. This last condition is not necessary, according to the Shafi'i school.
17. *Mughni,* p. 72; Kasani, op. cit.; *Mudawwanah,* vol. IV, p. 399; Haytami, *Tuhfat al-Muhtaj,* vol. IX, p. 115.
18. See above, chapter I, and Shalabi, *Al-Fiqh al-Islami,* p. 207.
19. Kasani, *Badai',* vol. VII, p. 50; *Mughni,* vol. IX, p. 64; *Al-Rawd al-Nadir,* vol. IV, p. 470 ff.
20. Zurqani's commentary on *Mukhtasar Khalil,* vol. VIII, pp. 99–100; Bajirmi, op. cit., p. 139; *Muhalla,* vol. XI, p. 176–181.
21. *Al-Rawd al-Nadir,* p. 473.
22. Kasani, op. cit.
23. Jassas, *Ahkam al-Qur'an,* vol. II, p. 429; see also pp. 427–428.
24. *Mughni,* vol. IX, p. 65; Kasani, op. cit., pp. 49–50; 'Uda, op. cit., vol. II, pp. 433–435; *Al-Rawd al-Nadir,* pp. 473–474.
25. Kasani, op. cit.; 'Uda, op.cit., p. 436.
26. Kasani, op. cit.; Mughni, p. 67; 'Uda, op. cit., p. 436.
27. Kasani, op. cit., p. 52; Ibn Nujaym, *Al-Ashbah wal-Nazai'r,* vol. II, p. 164; Khalil, *Mukhtasar,* with the commentary of Zurqani, p. 100; Mughni, op. cit. pp. 68–69.
28. Shu'rani, *Mizan,* vol. II, p. 137; *Mughni,* op. cit., p. 80; Shalabi, *Al-Fiqh al-Islami,* pp. 206–210.
29. *Mughni,* vol. IX, p. 65; Shafi'i, *Umm,* vol. VII, p. 141; *Fath al-Qadir,* vol. IV, pp. 158–159.

30. *Fath al-Qadir.*
31. During the time of the hajj in 1957, two married persons committed adultery and afterwards confessed it. They were stoned to death after the day of 'Arafat. This case was brought to my attention by many eye-witnesses who were there during the hajj, but no official records are available.
32. *Muhalla,* vol. IX, pp. 426–429.
33. *Badai' al-Sanai'*, vol. VII, p. 52; Baji, *Muntaqa,* vol. V, p. 186; *Mughni,* vol. IX, pp. 78–79.
34. *Mugni; Muntaqa;* 'Uda, op. cit., vol. II, p. 431, where *Muhadhdhab,* vol. II, p. 320, is cited.
35. *Al-Turuq al-Hukmiya,* pp. 210–217.
36. 'Uda, op. cit., pp. 431–432, where *Sharh al-Azhar,* vol. IV, p. 320, is quoted.
37. Ibn al-Qayyim, *Al-Turuq al-Hukmiyya,* p. 7; Ibn Farhun, *Tabsirah,* vol. II, p. 97.
38. Ibn Farhun, op. cit.
39. Ibid., p. 97.
40. Anderson, *Islamic Law in Africa,* p. 194.
41. Ibn Farhun, op. cit., p. 96; Ibn al-Qayyim, *I'lam al-Muwaqq'in,* vol. III, pp. 20–21.
42. A well-documented view that it is not, is expressed in *Al-Ibadiya fi Mawkib al-Tarikh* by Shaikh 'Ali Yahya Mu'ammar, vol. I, pp. 19–35. A more advanced discussion of this topic is to be found in *Studies in Ibadism,* by Dr. 'Amr Khalifa Ennami, pp. 9–43.
43. Atfayyish, *Sharh al-Nil,* vol. VII, pp. 548 ff.
44. Ibrahim, *Al-Qisas,* pp. 225–227, where the famous Egyptian Hanafi jurist, Shaikh Ahmad Ibrahim, is quoted from his book, *Turuq al-Ithbat al-Shar'iya.*
45. Ibn al-Qayyim, *Al-Turuq al-Hukmiyya,* p. 13.
46. Ibrahim, *Al-Qisas,* pp. 226–227.
47. Ibid., pp. 226-227.
48. Ibn Farhun, op. cit., pp. 111–112, where he quotes Qarafi in *Dhakhira,* his unpublished work on Maliki law; cf. Coulson, *A History of Islamic Law,* pp. 127–128.
49. Ibn al-Qayyim, op. cit., p. 15.

CONCLUSION

The ISLAMIC PENAL SYSTEM
AND
CONTEMPORARY MUSLIM SOCIETIES

Thus far we have dealt with the theory of punishment in Islamic law in an attempt to understand its main characteristics and underlying principles. The findings of this reasearch may be summarized by saying that Islamic law possesses a unique concept of punishment, a concept which in a sense cares very little for the criminal and his reform, and concentrates on preventing the commission of offences. This relates to that part of the penal system in Islamic law known as *hadd* punishments. In this area nothing is left to the legislator in the Muslim society; he cannot add anything to, subtract anything from, any of the rules laid down in the Qur'an and the Sunna relating to these punishments. Equally noteworthy is the Islamic manner of dealing with the crime of homicide, with its dualistic notion of punishment for a crime and compensation for a tort. Thus, the concept of *ta'zir,* or discretionary punishments, with the wide authority given to the ruler or legislator to establish crimes and their punishments, and with its direct concern with public morality, presents a permanent base on which the needs of the Muslim society can be met.

On the other hand the restrictions relating to inflicting the punishments, especially *hadd* punishments, in terms of difficulty of proof, recommendation of forgiveness, and the possibility of repentance, greatly limit the number of cases in which these punishments can be applied.

It can be generally said that punishment in Islamic law is primarily based on the concept of deterrence and retribution, but scope exists for reformative elements as well, particularly within the provisions of *ta'zir.*

134

However, in connection with the theory of punishment, the most controversial aspect discussed in contemporary Islamic circles is the possibility of applying the Islamic penal system in modern societies. Those who are involved in the dispute comprise two groups, one of which may be called "the advocates" of the application of the Islamic penal system, and the other may be called "the opponents." The discussion has not always been objective, for the opponents often accuse the advocates of being backward, narrow-minded, reactionary, and even barbarous. At the same time, the advocates are not less aggressive than their attackers; their list of accusations includes lack of faith, ignorance, and being under foreign, particularly Western, influence.

Apart from this exchange of accusations, both parties present a considerable variety of evidence for and against the case. The advocates, to defend their view, adduce many arguments, of which the two most important are the following: that the Islamic penal system is a part of the law of God which must be obeyed and enforced, and that the application of this system has proven to be successful in the past, as well as in modern times. Here they usually quote the example of Saudi Arabia, to which we have already referred.[1] As a matter of fact, both these arguments are correct, but the question is whether or not they justify the application of the Islamic penal system in contemporary Muslim societies.

On the other hand, the most important arguments against the case are that the penal system known to Islamic law is not, like other Islamic legal rules, of any use to present-day society because of its antiquity and lack of sophistication, and that the Islamic penal system in particular cannot be applied today as it is very severe, barbarous, and inhuman. No doubt the punishments recognized in Islamic law are very severe, but all the other allegations have been adequately replied to by the other side. However, it is not my intention here to go through all the details of this discussion, but simply to state briefly its main points in order to approach the problem.

In dealing with the application of the Islamic penal system, the starting point is the understanding of its place within the Islamic legal framework as a whole, or rather within Islam itself. It is well known that Islam provides a complete system for regulating every aspect of human life. The rules, obligations, injunctions, and prohibitions laid down by, or derived from, the Qur'an and Sunna produce a complete picture of the Muslim community from which no part can be removed without the rest being damaged. Equally, no isolated part of this scheme can make any sense or be of any use.

Within any legal system the philosophy of punishment is an integral part of the system which cannot be understood or applied except within its principles, in order to protect the values recognized by it. If this is correct, and it is undoubtedly correct, then it must be completely wrong to borrow the penal philosophy of one legal system and adapt it to another which is based on different principles and values, or, in relation to the issue at hand, to apply the concept of punishment laid down by Islamic law to a community in which any part of the Islamic scheme of life is lacking.

To turn to contemporary Muslim societies, one can hardly say that the Islamic way of life is adopted among them, or even well-understood. There is no exception to this statement, even in the widely-cited examples of some Muslim countries. Again, this is not the place to go into details, but anyone who has even a superficial knowledge of Muslim societies would agree with this .

Its is therefore nonsense to say that we must apply the Islamic penal system to present-day Muslim societies in their present circumstances. It is nonsense to amputate the thief's hand when he has no means of support but stealing. It is nonsense to punish in any way for *zina* (let alone to stone to death) in a community where everything invites and encourages unlawful sexual relationships.[2] Above all, it is nonsense to say that the penal code now in operation in a country such as Egypt is almost legitimate, under the doctrine of *ta'zir* recognized in Islamic law. Such a code simply has no connection with Islamic law and does not seek its legitimacy in the recognition of it, but in its suitability to the present circumstances of the society.[3] Those who try to justify some of the current systems in Muslim countries only prove their lack of understanding of the Islamic concept of life as laid down in the Qur'an, the Sunna, and the scholars' teachings.

From this perspective, i.e., the impossibility of isolating any part or parts of the Islamic scheme of life, one can say that the application of the Islamic penal system under present circumstances would not lead to the achievement of the ends recommended by this system. This leads us to consider two points made by the advocates of its application. The first is that the Islamic penal system has proved successful in the past as well as the present in preventing crime, or at least in minimizing the crime rate. As for the past, although one of its great advocates claims that "the Islamic penal code was in vogue up to the beginning of the nineteenth century,"[4] this claim can hardly be proved. Abu Yusuf, the second founder of the

Hanafi school tells us in his famous text, *Al-Kharaj,* about the extent of the application of the Islamic penal system during the era of Harun al-Rashid, the Abbasid Caliph. His statement leaves the reader with the clear understanding that by his time, the Islamic penal system was far from being enforced.[5] Abu Yusuf died in the year 182 A.H. This means that in less than two centuries after the Prophet's time circumstances had made it necessary to relax the enforcement of the Islamic penal system. This was due to the fact that the society for which this system was framed no longer existed after the widespread expansion of Islam among peoples of totally different values. It is the very same consideration, that is, the non-existence of the society visualized by Islam, which leads us to say that the application of the Islamic penal system today would not achieve its aim. The well-known example of its successful application in Saudi Arabia can only be used as evidence for this view.

The second point we may consider is the claim that the Islamic penal system is preferable to any other because Islam, and the Muslim jurists, discovered and legalized all the theories known to modern penal codes and legislations. This early advancement, say the advocates, is a point in favour of the application of this penal system. This point has often inspired articles, speeches, and even text books. To me it has no relevance to the application of the penal system of Islamic law. It may be of great value in research concerned with legal or social history, but it certainly has nothing to do with the application of a legal system. The only justification for adopting one legal system and not another is that the one in force provides the community with all possible "good" and protects it from all possible "bad." Without doubt the Islamic legal system had such qualifications in the past, when circumstances were appropriate for its enforcement. Moreover there is no doubt, at least to Muslims, that the will of God as revealed in the Qur'an and the trustworthy Sunna has an eternal value and the capacity to safeguard the community's interests. But first, before we can demand the enforcement of the Islamic penal system, it must be proved beyond the slightest shadow of a doubt that the Islamic society visualized in the Qur'an and the Sunna has become an existing fact.

Futhermore, it must be remembered that Islamic law is an ideal legal system, i.e., it is not a law of custom which grew up within the society in which it was applied; rather it is a legal system which was formulated in order to realize an ideal society, the Islamic society. This idealism is clear enough from the Qur'anic injunctions and prohibitions concerned with the social life of Muslims. Nevertheless, it is even clearer in the jurists' works, not only on social but also on legal and even political issues. Islamic law measures the realities in society according to Islamic standards and approves or disapproves them. This is not because of what people do or abstain from doing, but because things are intrinsically "good" or "bad." Apart from the rules of public interest *(maslaha),* neccessity *(darorah),* misuse of right *(isaat ist'mal al-haqq),* and other similar rules, this emphasis on ideal concepts is the general tendency in Islamic law. One can therefore say again that if that ideal society does not exist, Islamic law as expressed in the jurists' manual cannot be applied. Even historically this was so, as for example in the establishment of the court of the official in charge of crimes *(wali al-jara'im)* who was to deal with criminal cases on a different basis both in matters of procedure and substance than the usual court of the *qadi.*[6]

We conclude, therefore, that the Islamic penal system, or rather Islamic law, is to be applied only within the above-mentioned Islamic society. Whenever that society comes into existence, the Islamic legal system will be able to operate without any need for "the advocates" and in spite of all the objections of "the opponents." Whether or not this society will come into being is a matter beyond any personal judgment. But it is the duty of every capable Muslim to work as hard as he can to achieve a state of affairs in which Islamic law governs every Muslim society.

NOTES

1. Another example which may be referred to is that of Kuwait. The Islamic penal system, including *hadd* punishments, was theoretically enforced there until 1960, when the first penal code was formulated. The only exception to this was *hadd* punishment for theft, which had been set aside by an order of the late Shaikh Jabir al-Ahmad in 1931. This order was given according to a *fatwa* (formal legal opinion) issued by the then *mufti* of Kuwait. This information was given to me in a letter of reply from Major General A. F. Thuaini, the Under-Secretary of State for the Interior of Kuwait, to whom I am very much indebted.
2. A similar view was expressed by the late Abul al-A'la Mawdudi, in his book, *Islamic Law and Constitution,* pp. 53-59.
3. Compare, for example, Abu Zahra, *Al-Jarimah wal 'Uquba,* p. 126.
4. Mawdudi, op. cit., p. 65.
5. *Al-Kharaj,* pp. 149–152.
6. For further details, see Shalabi, *Al-Fiqh al-Islami Bayn al-Mithaliya wal-Waqi'ya,* pp. 6–19; Coulson; *Conflicts and Tensions in Islamic Jurisprudence,* pp. 58-76. Although each one of these two writers has approached the subject in a different manner, they both contribute to it.

BIBLIOGRAPHY

ARABIC SOURCES:

A. Islamic Law

1. The Qur'an and Commentaries:

— 'Abd al-Rahman, 'Aisha, *Al-Qur'an wal-Tafsir al-'Asri*, Cairo, 1970.
— Ibn al-'Arabi, Muhammad b. 'Abd Allah, *Ahkam al Qur'an*, Cairo (n.d.).
— Ibn al-Jawzi, Jamal al-Din 'Abd al-Rahman, *Zad al-Masir fi 'Ilm al-Tafsir*, Damascus, 1965.
— Ibn Kathir, Isma'il b. 'Omar, called 'Imad al-Din, *Tafsir al-Qur'an al-'Azim*, Cairo (n.d.).
— Jassas, Abu Bakr Ahmad b. 'Ali, *Ahkam al-Qur'an*, Istanbul, 1355 A.H.
— Mawdudi, Abu al-A'la, *Tafsir Surat al-Nur*, translated from Urdu, Damascus, 1959.
— Qurtubi, Muhammad b. Ahmad al-Ansari, *Al-Jami' li Ahkam al-Qur'an*, Cairo, 1942.
— Qutb, Sayed, *Fi Zilal al-Qur'an*, 7th Ed., Kuwait, 1967.
— Rida, al-Sayed Muhammad Rashid, *Tafsir al-Manar*, 10-vol. unfinished commentary on the Qur'an based on the views of Shaikh Muhammad 'Abdu, Cairo (n.d.).
— Suyuty, Jalal al-Din 'Abd al-Rahman, *Al-Itqan fi 'Ulum al-Qur'an*, Cairo, 1951.
— Tabari, Abu Ja'far Muhammad b. Jarir, *Jami' al-Bayan fi Tafsir al-Qur'an*. Cairo (n.d.).

2. Collections and Treatises of Hadith:

— Abu Dawud, Sulayman b. al-Ash'ath, *Al-Sunan*, a collection of Hadith, India, 1323 A.H.
— Albani, Muhammad Nasir al-Din, a commentary on *Mukhtasar Sahih Muslim*, by Mundhiri, Kuwait, 1969.
— A commentary on *Mishkat al—Masabih*, by Tabrizi, Damascus, 1961.
— Bayhaqi, Ahmad b. al-Husain b. 'Ali, *Al-Sunan al-Kubra*, Hyderabad, India, 1354 A.H.
— Bukhari, Muhammad b. Isma'il, *Kitab al-Sahih*, Cairo, 1939.
— Ibn Hajar, Ahmad b. 'Ali b. Muhammad, *Fath al-Bari*, a commentary on *Sahih al-Bukhari*, published with the above book.
— Ibn Kathir, Isma'il b. 'Omar, *Mukhtasar 'Ulum al-Hadith*, with the commentary of Ahmad Shakir, Cairo (n.d.).
— Ibn Qayyim al-Jawziyah, Muhammad b. Abu Bakr, called b. al-Qayyim, *Zad al-Ma'ad*, Cairo, 1379 A.H.
— Muslim, Abu al-Hussain b. al-Hajjaj al-Qushairi, *Kitab al-Sahih*, Istanbul (n.d.).
— Mundhiri, 'Abd al-'Azim b. 'Abd al-Qawi, *Mukhtasar Sahih Muslim*, with the commentary of Albani, Kuwait, 1969.
— Nawawi, Abu Zakariya Yahya b. Sharaf al-Din, commentary on Muslim, *Kitab al-Sahih*, Cairo (n.d.).
— Naysaburi, Muhammad b. 'Abd Allah, called al-Hakim, *Ma'rifat 'Ulum al-Hadith*, edited by Dr. Mu'zzam Husain, Beirut (n.d.).

139

— Sabiq, al-Sayed, *Fiqh al-Sunna*, Kuwait, 1968.
— Shawkani, Muhammad b. 'Ali, *Navl al-Awtar*. Cairo, 1357 A.H.
— Tabrizi, Wali al-Din Muhammad b. 'Abd Allah, *Mishkat al-Masabih*, with the commentary of Albani, Damascus, 1961.
— Tahawi, Ahmad b. Muhammad b. Salamah, *Sharh Ma'ani al-Athar*, India, 1929.
— Zubaydi, Ahmad b. Ahmad, called al-Husain b. al-Mubarak, *Al-Tajrid al-Sarih*, extract of Bukhari, *Kitab al-Sahih*, Beirut (n.d.).

3. Works on Usul al-Fiqh and Legal Principles:
— Baidawi, Nasir al-Din, *Minhaj al-Wusul ila 'Ilm al-Usul*, Cairo, 1326 A.H.
— Ibn Hazm, Abu Muhammad 'Ali, *Al-Ihkam fi Usul al-Ahkam*, Cairo, 1347 A.H.
— Ibn Nujaym, Zayn al-'Abidin Ibrahim, *Al-Ashbah wal-Naza'ir*, Cairo, 1290 A.H.
— Ibn al-Shat, Qasim b. 'Abd Allah, a commentary on Qarafi, *Kitab al-Furuq* (see below), called *Idrar al-Shuruq 'ala Anwaa' al-Furuq*.
— Khallaf, 'Abd al-Wahhab, *'Ilm Usul al-Fiqh*, 8th Ed., Kuwait, 1968.
— Nasafi, 'Abd Allah Ahmad b. Mahmud, *Manar al-Anwar fi Usul al-Fiqh*, Asitanah, 1315 A.H.
— Qarafi, Shihab al-Din al-'Abbas b. Ahmad, *Kitab al-Furuq al-Saniya*, Cairo, 1939.
— . . . . ., *Al-Ihkam fi Tamyeez al-Fatawa 'an al-Ahkam*, Damascus, 1967, edited by 'Abd al-Fattah Abu Ghuddah.
— Shafi'i, Muhammad b. Idris, *Kitab al- Risalah*, with the commentary of Shaikh Ahmad Shakir, Cairo, 1940.
— Shalabi, Shaikh Muhammad Mustafa, *Ta'lil al-Ahkam*, Al-Azhar University Press, Cairo, 1949.
— . . . . ., *Usul al-Fiqh*, Beirut, 1967.
— Shatibi, Ibrahim b. Musa al-Bakhmi, *Kitab al-Muwafaqat fi Usul al-Shari'a*, Cairo (n.d.).

4. Works of Different Schools of Law:
— 'Abbadi, Ibn Qasim, a commentary on *Tuhfat al-Muhtaj* (Sh), text by Haytami (see below), published with the original text, Cairo, 1938.
— Abu Ya'la, Muhammad b. al-Husain al-Farra', *Al-Ahkam al-Sultaniya* (B), Cairo, 1357 A.H.
— Abu Yusuf Ya'qub b. Ibrahim, *Kitab al-Kharaj* (H), Cairo, 1352 A.H.
— 'Adawi, Shaikh 'Ali, commentary on *Mukhtasar Khalil* (M), published with the commentary of Shaikh al-Khirshi (see below), Cairo, 1308 A.H.
— Ansari, Zakariya, *Sharh Rawd al-Talib* (Sh), Cairo (n.d.).
— . . . , a commentary on *Matn al-Bahjah* (Sh), by Ibn al-Wardi, Cairo, 1900.
— Atfayyish, Muhammad b. Yusuf, called al-Qutb, *Sharh al-Nil* (D), Cairo (n.d.).
— Bahuti, Mansur b. Yunus b. Idris, *Kashshaf al-Qina'* (B), a commentary on Hajawi's *Matn al-Iqna'* (see below), Riyadh (n.d.).
— Baji, Sulayman b. Khalaf b. Sa'd, *Al-Muntaqa Sharh al-Muwatta'* (M), Cairo (n.d.).
— Bajirmi, Sulayman b. 'Omar, *Tuhfat al-Habib 'ala Sharh al-Khatib* (Sh), Cairo, 1308 A.H.
— Dardir, Shaikh Ahmad, a commentary on *Mukhtasar Khalil* (M), Cairo (n.d.).
— Ghazali, Muhammad b. Muhammad, *Al-Wajiz* (Sh), Cairo (n.d.).
— Hajawi, Musa b. Ahmad b. Salim, *Al-Iqna'* (B), with the commentary of Bahuti (see above), Riyadh (n.d.).
— Hasani, al-'Abbas b. Ahmad, *Tatimmat al-Rawd al-Nadir*, (Zd), a fifth volume with which *Al-Rawd al-Nadir* (Zd) (see below, Siyaghi) is completed, Damascus, 1968.

— Haskafi, Muhammad b. 'Ali, called 'Ala al-Din, *Al-Durr al-Mukhtar* (H), in the margin of Ibn 'Abdin's *Al-Hashiya* (see below), Cairo, 1966.

— Hattab, Muhammad Muhammad 'Abd al-Rahman, a commentary on *Mukhtasar Khalil* (M), published with Mawwaq's commentary on the same text (see below).

— Haytami, Ahmad b. Muhammad b. Hajar, *Tuhfat al-Muhtaj ila Sharh al-Minhaj* (Sh), a commentary on Nawawi's *Minhaj al-Talibin*, Cairo (n.d.).

— Hilli, Najm al-Din Ja'far b. Hassan, called al-Muhaqqiq, *Sharai' al-Islam* (I), Beirut (n.d.).

— Ibn 'Abdin, Muhammad Amin, *Al-Hashiya* (H), a commentary on *Al-Durr al-Mukhtar* by Haskafi, published together, Cairo, 1966.

— ..., *Minhat al-Khaliq*, a commentary on *Al-Bahr al-Ra'iq* (H), of Ibn Nujaym (see below).

— Ibn Farhun, Ibrahim Shams al-Din Muhammad, *Tabsirat al-Hukkam* (M), Cairo, 1301 A.H.

— Ibn Hazm, 'Ali b. Muhammad, *Al-Muhalla* (Z), Beirut (n.d.).

— Ibn al-Humam, Kamal al-Din Muhammad, *Fath al-Qadir*, a commentary on *Al-Hidaya* (H), Cairo, 1316 A.H.

— Ibn Juzaiy, Muhammad b. Ahmad, *Qawanin al-Ahkam al-Shar'iya* (M), Beirut, 1968.

— Ibn Nujaym, Zayn al-'Abidin Ibrahim, *Al-Bahr al-Ra'iq Sharh Kanz al-Daqa'iq* (H) Cairo (n.d.).

— ...., *Risalah fi Iqamat al-Qadi al-Ta'zir* (H), appended to his *Al-Ashbah wal-Nazai'r*.

— Ibn Rushd, Abu al-Walid Muhammad b. Ahmad, called al-Hafid, *Bidayat al-Mujtahid* (M), Cairo, 1966.

— Kasani, 'Ala al-Din Abu Bakr b. Mas'ud, *Badai' al-Sanai'* (H), Cairo, 1910.

— Khalil, Abu al-Diya' b. Ishaq, *Mukhtasar* (M), with the commentary of Zurqani (see below), Cairo (n.d.)

— Khirshi, Abu 'Abd Allah Muhammad, a commentary on *Mukhtasar Khalil*, Cairo 1308 A.H.

— Kinani, 'Abd Allah b. 'Abd Allah, *Al-'Iqd al-Munazza lil-Hukkam* (M), in the margin of Ibn Farhun, Cairo, 1301 A.H.

— Malik, Ibn Anas al-Asbahi, *Kitab al-Muwatta'* (M), edited by M. F.' Abd al-Baqi,, Cairo, 1951.

— Mardawi, 'Ali b. Sulayman, *Al-Insaf fi Ma'rifat al-Rajih Min al-Khilaf* (B), Cairo, 1957.

— Mawardi, 'Ali b. Muhammad b. Habib, *Al-Ahkam al-Sultaniya* (Sh), Cairo, 1380 A.H.

— Mawwaq, Muhammad b. Yusuf, a commentary on *Mukhtasat Khalil* (M), published with the commentary of Hattab, Cairo, 1329 A.H.

— Mirghinani, 'Ali b. Abi Bakr, *Hidaya* (H), published with the commentary of Ibn al-Humam (see above).

— Muzani, Isma'il b. Yahya, *Mukhtasar al-Umm* (Sh), published with the Shafi'i's *Kitab al-Umm* (see below), Cairo, 1968.

— Nawawi, Yahya Sharaf al-Din, *Minhaj al-Talibin* (Sh), Cairo (n.d.).

— Ramli, Muhammad b. Abi al-'Abbas b. Hamza, *Nihayat al-Muhtaj ila Sharh al-Minhaj* (Sh), a commentary on *Minhaj al-Talibin* (see above), Cairo, 1938.

— Ruhaybani, Mustafa al-Suyuti, *Matalib Uli al-Nuha* (B), Damascus, 1961.

— Sa'di, Sa'd Allah b. 'Isa, called Sa'di Afandi and Sa'di Jelbi, a commentary on *Al-'Inaya* (H), this being a commentary on *Al-Hidaya* (see above), published with *Fath al-Qadir* of Ibn al-Humam.

— Sarakhsi, Muhammad b. Sahl, called Abu Bakr, *Mabsut* (H), Cairo, 1342 A.H.

— ..., *Al-Siyar* (H), India, 1335 A.H.

— Shafi'i, Muhammad b. Idris, *Kitab al-Umm* (Sh), Cairo, 1968.
— Shirazi, Ibn Ishaq, *Mudhdhab* (Sh), Cairo (n.d.).
— Shirbini, Muhammad al-Khatib, *Mughni al-Muhtaj* (Sh), a commentary on Nawawi's *Minhaj*, Cairo, 1308 A.H.
— Shirwani, 'Abd al-Hamid, commentary on Haytami's *Tuhfat al-Muhtaj* (Sh), published with the same text, Cairo, 1938.
— Shubramulsi, 'Ali b. 'Ali, a commentary on *Sharh al-Minhaj* of al-Ramli (Sh), Cairo, 1292 A.H.
— Siyaghi, al-Husain b. Ahmad, called Sharaf al-Din, *Al-Rawd al-Nadir* (Zd), a commentary on *Majmu' al-Fiqh al-Kabir* by Imam Zayd, Damascus, 1968.
— Tannukhi, Sahnun b. Said, *Al-Mudawwanah al-Kubran* (M), Cairo, 1323 A. H.
— Tarabulsi, 'Ali b. Khalil, called 'Ala'al-Din, *Mu'in al-Huk*am (H), Cairo, 1300 A. H.
— Zayla'i, Othman b. 'Ali, called Fakhr al-Din, Tabyeen al-Haqai'q, (H), a commentary on Kanz al Daqai'q, (H), pub. with it, Cairo, 1313 A.H.

5. *Comparative Islamic Law:*

— Ibn Qayyim al-Jawziya, Muhammad b. Abi Bakr, called Ibn al-Qayyim, Hadi al-Arwah, Cairo, 1938.
— ..., I'lam al-Muwaqq'in, Cairo, 1955.
— ..., Ighathat al-Lahfan Min Masayed al-Shytan, Cairo, 1939.
— ..., al-Turuq al-Hukmiya fil-Siyasat al-Shari'iya, Cairo, 1960.
— Ibn Qudamah, 'Abd Allah b. Ahmad b. Muhammad, al-Mughni, Cairo, al-Manar Ed. (n.d.), another Ed. 1969.
— Ibn Taymiyya, Ahmad 'Abd Al-Halim b. Majd al-Din, al-Siyasat al-Shari'iya, Cairo, 1952.
— ..., al-Hisba fil-Islam, Cairo, (n.d.).
— ..., al-Sarim al-Maslul 'Ala Shatim al-Rasul, India, 1322 A.H.
— Shu'rani, 'Abd al-Wahhab Ahmad, Mizan, Cairo, 1318 A.H.

---

* Muhalla by Ibn Hazm and al-Rawd al-Nadir by Siyaghi are actually texts of comparative Islamic law, but in this thesis they were used for Zahiri and Zaydi views respectively, so I referred to both of them among the works for the law schools.

6. *Modern Writing:*

— Abu Haif, 'Ali Sadiq, *Al-Diya*, thesis, Cairo, 1932.
— Abu Zahra, Shaikh Muhammad, *Al-Jarimah wal-'Uquba*, Cairo (n.d.)
— ..., *Falsafat al-'Uquba*, Cairo, 1966.
— 'Amer, 'Abd al-'Aziz, *Al-Ta'zir fil-Shari'a al-Islamiya*, 3rd ed., thesis, Cairo, 1957.
— Darwazat, Muhammad 'Izzat, *Al-Dustur al-Qur'ani fi Shu'un al-Hayah*, Cairo, 1956.
— Ibrahim, Ahmad Muhammad, *Al-Qisas fil-Shari'a al-Islamiya*, thesis, Cairo, 1944.
— Mawdudi, Abu al-A'la, *Nazariyat al-Islam al-Siyasiyya*, translated fron Urdu, Damascus, 1967.
— Shalabi, Shaikh Muhammad Mustafa, *Al-Fiqh al-Islami Bayn al-Mithaliya al-Waqi'ya*, Alexandria, 1960.
— ..., *Al-Madkhal li Dirasat al-Fiqh al-Islami*, 8th Ed., Beirut, 1969.
— Shaltut, Shaikh Mahmud, *Al-Islam, 'Aqida wa Shari'a*, Cairo, 1964.
— Sharabasi, Ahmad, *Al-Qisas fil-Islam*, Cairo, 1954.
— 'Uda, 'Abd al-Qadir, *Al-Tashri' al-Jina'i al-Islami Muqaranan bi al-Qanun al-Wad'l*, Cairo, vol.I: 1959, vol II: 1960.

B. Secondary Works:
— 'Ashmawi, Hassan, *Al-Fard al-'Arabi wa Mushkilat al-Hukm*, Beirut, 1970,

143 BIBLIOGRAPHY

— Baghdadi, 'Abd al-Qahir b. Tahir, *Al-Farq Bayn al-Firaq*, Cairo, 1965.
— Bustani, Amin Afram, *Sharh Qanun al-'Uqubat al-Misri*, Cairo, 1894.
— Damiri, Muhammad b. 'Isa, called Kamal al-Din, *Hayat al-Hayawan*, Cairo (n.d.).
— Ibn 'Abd Rabbih, Ahmad b. Muhammad, *Al-'Iqd al-Farid*, Cairo, 1940.
— Ibn Hazm, 'Ali b. Ahmad, *Al-Fisal fi al-Milal wal-Nihal*, Cairo (n.d.).
— Jahiz, 'Amr b. Bahr, *Kitab al-Hayawan, Cairo*, 1356 A.H.
— Keshki, 'Abd al-Rahim, *Al-Mirath al-Muqaran*, Baghdad, 1969.
— Khalifa, Ahmad Muhammad, *Al-Nazariya al-'Amma lil-Tajrim*, thesis, Cairo, 1959.
— Mu'ammar, Shaikh 'Ali Yahya, *Al-Ibadiya fi Mawkib al-Tarikh*, Cairo, 1964.
— Qutb, Muhammad, *Manhaj al-Tarbiya al-Islamiyya*, 3rd Ed., Beirut, 1967.
— Shatibi, Ibrahim b. Musa al-Lakhmi, *Al-I'tisam*, Cairo, 1332 A.H.
— Uda, 'Abd al-Qadir, *Al-Islam wa Awda'una al-Siyasiyya*, 2nd Ed., Beirut, 1967.

ENGLISH SOURCES
A. Islamic *Law*:
— Ali, Yusuf, *The Holy Qu'ran, Translation and Commentary*, New York, 1946.
— Ali, Muhammad, *The Religion of Islam*, Cairo, 1967.
— Anderson, J.N.D., *Islamic Law in Africa*, London, 1954.
— ...., "Homicide in Islamic Law," *Bulletin of the School of Oriental and African Studies*, London, 1951.
— Arberry, A.J., *The Qur'an Interpreted, a Translation of the Qur'an*, Oxford, 1969.
— Bassiouni, Cherif, "Islam: Concept, Law and World Habeas Corpus," *Rutgers-Camden Law Journal*, 1968.
— Coulson, N.J., *A History of Islamic Law*, Edinburgh University Press, 1971.
— ..., *Conflicts and Tensions in Islamic Jurisprudence*, Chicago, 1969.
— ..., *Succession in the Muslim Family*, Cambridge University Press 1971.
— ..., "The State and Individual in Islamic Law," *International and Comparative Law Quarterly*, Vol. IV, January 1957.
— Ennami, 'Amr Khalifa, *Studies in Ibadism*, Cambridge, 1971 (unpublished doctoral thesis).
— Fazlul Karim, A.M., *Al-Hadis, a Translation of Mishkat al-Masabih of Tabrizi*, Calcutta, 1938.
— Goldziher, Ignaz, *Muslim Studies*, translated from the German by C.R. Barber and S.M. Stern, vol I., London, 1967.
— Levy, Reuben, *The Social Structure of Islam*, Cambridge, 1969.
— Mawdudi, Abu al-A'la, *Islamic Law and Constitution* (translated from Urdu bu Khurshid Ahmad), 3rd Ed., Lahore, 1967.
— Pickthall, M. M. *The Meaning of the Glorious Qur'an, a Translation of the Qur'an*, Karachi (nd).
— Schacht, J., *An Introduction to Islamic Law*, Oxford, 1964.
— Zwemer, S. M. *The Law of Apostasy in Islam*, London, 1924.

B. Other Sources
— Abraham, Gerald, *Morality and the Law, London, 1971*.
— Baylis, C.A., "Immorality, Crime and Treatment," *Philosophical Perspective of Punishment*, edited by E.H. Madden and others, New York, 1968.
— Blanshard, B., "Retribution Revisited," *Philosophical Perspective of Punishment*, edited by E.H. Madden and others, New York, 1968.
— Bloom-Cooper, L., *The A G Murderer*, Penguin London, 1963.

— Canham, H.A., *The Nature of Punishment*, unpublished doctoral thesis, London, 1966.
— Clark, M., "The Moral Gradation of Punishment, *Philosophical Quarterly*, April, 1971.
— Clerk and Lindsell, *Torts*, edited by A.L. Armitage and others, 13th Ed., Sweet and Maxwell, London, 1969.
— Cross, R., and Jones, P.A., *Introduction to Criminal Law*, 6th Ed., London, 1968.
— Devlin, Lord Patrick, *The Enforcement of Morals*, 3rd Ed., Oxford University Press, 1969.
— Ducasse, C.J., "Philosophy and Wisdom in Punishment and Reward," *Philosophical Perspective of Punishment*, edited by E.H. Madden and others, New York, 1968.
— East, Sir Norwood, *Society and the Criminal*, H.M.S.O., London, 1960.
— Ehrlich, J.W., *The Holy Bible and the Law*, New York, 1962.
— Elkin, W.A., *The English Penal System*, London, 1957.
— Fitzgerald, P.J., *Criminal Law and Punishment*, Oxford, 1962.
— Fleming, J.G., *The Law of Tort*, 3rd Ed., Sydney, 1965.
— Foot, Paul, *Was Hanratty Guilty?*, London, 1971.
— Fry, M., *Arms of the Law*, London, 1951.
— Fuller, L.L., *The Morality of Law*, Revised Ed., London, 1969.
— Goodhart, A.L., *English Law and the Moral Law*, London, 1953.

— . . . , "The Shaw Case: The Law and Public Morals," *Law Quarterly Review*, Vol. 77, 1961.
— Hall, J. "Science and Reform in Criminal Law," *University of Pennsylvania Law Review*, Philadelphia, 1952.
— Harris, *Harris' Criminal Law*, edited by Anthony Hooper, 21st Ed., London, 1968.
— Hart, H.L.A., *Law, Liberty and Morality*, London, 1969.
— . . . , *The Morality of the Criminal Law*, London, 1965.
— Hibbert, C., *The Roots of Evil*, London, 1966.
— The Holy Bible, Nelson Edition, London, 1965.
— Honderich, T., *Punishment: the Supposed Justification*, London, 1971.
— Jones, H., *Crime and the Penal System*, 3rd Ed., London, 1965.
— Kenny, *Outlines of Criminal Law*, Edited by J.W.C. Turner, 17th Ed., Cambridge 1958.
— Kessel, N., and Walton H., *Alcoholism*, 3rd Rev. Ed., London, 1969.
— Lessnoff, M., "Two Jusifications of Punishment," *The Philosophical Quarterly*, April, 1971.
— Lloyd, Lord, *The Idea of Law*, 4th Rev. Ed., London 1970.
— Longford, Lord Pakenham, *The Idea of Punishment*, London, 1961.
— Mannheim, H., *Comparative Criminology*, London, 1965.
— Mitchell, B., *Law, Morality and Religion in A Secular Society*, London, 1970.
— Molteno, O., *The Rules Behind the Rule of Law*, University of Natal, 1965.
— Page, L., *Crime and the Community*, London, 1937.
— Rolph, C.H., *Common Sense about Crime and Punishment*, London, 1961.
— Smart, Frances, *Neurosis and Crime*, edited by B.C. Brown, London, 1970.
— Wolfgang, M.E., *Patterns in Criminal Homicide*, New York, 1966.
— Williams, Hall, *The English Penal System in Transition, London, 1970*.
— Winfield, *On Tort*, edited by J. Jolowicz and E. Lewis, 8th Ed., London, 1967.

C. *Official Publications:*
— *Capital Punishment, the Royal Commission Report on*, H.M.S.O., Cmd. 8832, 1949 1953, reprinted 1965.

— *Compensation of Victims of Crimes of Violence*, *Report on,* H.M.S.O., Cmd. 1406 and 2323, reprinted 1961 and 1964.
— *Corporal Punishments, Report of the Departmental Committe* on H.M S.O., Cmd 5684, 1963.
— *Drunken, Habitual Offenders, Report of the Working Party on*, London, H.M.S.O., 1971.
— *The Sentence of the Court, a Hand Book for Courts on the Treatment of Offenders*, H.M.S.O., 1970.
— Timothy J. Evans, *The Results of the Inquiry Led by Mr. Scott Henderson*, Q.C. Report of the case H.M.S.O., Cmd. 8896, 1853.
— *Treatment of Offenders, Report of the Advisory Council on*, H.M.S.O., Cmd. 1213, 1961.
— U.N. Secretariat, *Working Paper for the United Nations Conference on Prevention of Crime and Treatment of Offenders*, Organization of Research for Policy Development, New York, 1970.
— *The Standard Minimum Rules for the Treatment of Prisoners*, New York, 1970.
— . . . , *Final Report of the Preparatory Arab Conference Organized by the U.N. and the League of Arab States*, Kuwait, 1970.

Acts and Codes
— Criminal Damage Act, 1971.
— Criminal Justice Act, 1967.
— Criminal Justice Bill, 1971, (Now Criminal Justice Act, 1972).
— Death Penalty Act, The Abolition of, 1965.
— Penal Code, The Egyptian, 1873 and 1937.
— Penal Code of Kuwait, 1960.
— Prevention of Crime Act, 1908.

Encyclopaedias:
— *The Encyclopaedia of Islam*, London, Vol II: 1928 Vol. III: 1936.
— *The Encyclopaedia of Islamic Jurisprudence*, Kuwait (preliminary edition in Arabic, 1969).
— *The Jewish Encyclopaedia*, London, 1901.

Dictionaries:
— *Law Dictionary*, by Mozley and Whiteley, 8th ed., London, 1970.
— *Lisan al-'Arab*, by Ibn Manzur, Muhammad b. al-Mukarram, Cairo (n.d.).
— *Mu'jam Maqayis al-Lughat*, by Ibn Faris, Ahmed, Cairo, 1369 A.H.
— *Mukhtar al-Sihah*, by 'Abd al-Hamid, Muhammad, and al-Subki, 'Abd al-Latif, Cairo, 1353 A.H.

Newspapers:
— *The Times*, London.